THE NONPROFIT ENTREPRENEUR
Creating Ventures to Earn Income

The
NONPROFIT ENTREPRENEUR

Creating Ventures To Earn Income

Edited by

EDWARD SKLOOT

The Foundation Center

Library of Congress Cataloging-in-Publication Data

The Nonprofit entrepreneur : creating ventures to earn income / edited
  by Edward Skloot.
    p.   cm.
    Bibliography: p.
    Includes index.
    ISBN 0-87954-239-X
    1. Corporations, Nonprofit—Finance. 2. Corporations, Nonprofit-
United States—Finance. 3. Fund raising. I. Skloot, Edward.
II. Foundation Center.
HG4027.65.N66 1988
658.1'5—dc19   87-36494

To Suzanne and Joseph Aaron Skloot
and to
William M. Dietel and Benjamin R. Shute, Jr.

Contributors

ELLEN ARRICK has been a program investment officer in the Office of Program Related Investments at the Ford Foundation since 1982. Her portfolio of investments includes projects in rural and urban economic development, education, and the arts. Prior to coming to the Ford Foundation, she worked as a loan officer in the Corporate Division at Chemical Bank. She holds an M.B.A. from the Columbia University Graduate School of Business and a B.A. from Brown University.

NANCY E. HAYCOCK is associate director of the Nonprofit Coordinating Committee of New York. She has worked extensively with and for small nonprofit organizations, including the Association for Neighborhood and Housing Development (as deputy director) and the Community Resource Exchange (as senior associate). She holds an M.A. in urban affairs and policy analysis from the New School and a B.A. from Rutgers University.

BRUCE R. HOPKINS is a lawyer with the Washington, D.C., office of Baker and Hostetler. He specializes in the representation of nonprofit organizations. He is author of *The Law of Tax-Exempt Organizations* (5th ed., 1987), editor of *The Nonprofit Counsel* (monthly newsletter), and is on the faculty of The George Washington University National Law Center, where he teaches the course on tax-exempt organizations. He recently served as chairman of the Committee on Exempt Organizations, Section on Taxation, American Bar Association.

ELLIOTT N. LANG is president of Museum Quality Services, Inc., a New York-based consulting firm that works with nonprofit institutions to develop their retail marketing potential. Mr. Lang has more than 25 years of experience in retailing, as executive vice-president of Saks Fifth Avenue and president of Brentano's. He is a graduate of Amherst College, magna cum laude, a member of Phi Beta Kappa, and serves as a director of the Greater New York Councils, Boy Scouts of America.

CHRISTOPHER H. LOVELOCK is a principal of Christopher Lovelock and Associates, a consulting and educational firm in Cambridge, Massachusetts. He was a professor at the Harvard Business School from 1973–1984 and has also taught at Stanford University and the University of California at Berkeley. He is author or coauthor of numerous articles and nine books, including *Services Marketing* (Prentice-Hall, 1984). With his long-time collaborator, Charles B. Weinberg, he wrote *Marketing Challenges* (McGraw-Hill, 1985) and *Public and Nonprofit Marketing: Cases and Readings* (Scientific Press, 1984). In 1988 they will publish a second edition of their book, *Marketing for Public and Nonprofit Managers* (also with Scientific Press). A native of Great Britain, Lovelock obtained a B.Com. and an M.A. in economics from the University of Edinburgh, and later obtained his M.B.A. from Harvard and Ph.D. from Stanford University.

CYNTHIA W. MASSARSKY is Director of Marketing and Licensing of the Free to Be Foundation. Before joining the foundation, she was vice-president of New Ventures, a New York consulting firm that works with nonprofit executives to strengthen their organizations' management, business, and marketing functions. There, she specialized in market research, financial analysis and planning, and new business development. Prior to coming to the firm, Ms. Massarsky served as director of development at The Foundation Center and, before that, as the director of the nation's first after-school program for children in grades 3–6. Ms. Massarsky received her M.B.A. from Cornell University Graduate School of Business and Public Administration. She holds a B.A. in psychology from Simmons College.

EDWARD SKLOOT is founder (1980) and President of New Ventures, a New York consulting firm that works with nonprofit executives to strengthen their organizations' management, business, and marketing functions. He served in a variety of public- and private-sector positions, including that of deputy administrator of Parks, Recreation, and Cultural Affairs of New York City; deputy commissioner of mental hygiene of New York State, and education director of the 92nd Street YM/YWHA. His venturing work has helped create numerous products and services, including the American Red Cross' first-aid "pillow," Planned Parenthood's ® condom, and the original TKTS booth on Broadway. He has published widely in such journals as the *Harvard Business Review,* the *Entrepreneurial Economy, Nonprofit World,* and *Foundation News.* He received a B.A. from Union College, a Masters of International Affairs from Columbia University, and was a Fulbright Fellow in India.

CHARLES B. WEINBERG is Alumni Professor of Marketing at the University of British Columbia. He taught previously at Stanford University, London (U.K.) Business School, and New York University. He and Christopher Lovelock have worked together for more than 15 years and have written many articles and books together, including, most recently, *Marketing for Public and Nonprofit Managers* and *Marketing Challenges: Cases and Exercices.* He has been actively involved in the implementation of innovative approaches to nonprofit marketing and currently serves as vice president of marketing for the Vancouver Symphony Orchestra. He earned a Sc.B. from Brown University, an M.B.A. from Harvard University, and a Ph.D. from Columbia University.

WIM WIEWEL is director of the University of Illinois' Center for Urban Economic Development at the School of Urban Planning and Public Policy in Chicago. He specializes in studies of organizational structure, technology, and industrial development. He has published technical reports and manuals on market-feasibility studies, business activities by nonprofit organizations, and specific neighborhood development projects. Before joining UICUED in 1979, he conducted research on the Housing Assistance Supply Experiment for the RAND Corporation. He holds degrees in sociology and urban planning from the University of Amsterdam in the Netherlands and a Ph.D. in sociology from Northwestern University.

Contents

INTRODUCTION

The Growth of, and Rationale for, Nonprofit Enterprise

EDWARD SKLOOT

UNTIL RECENTLY, the term *nonprofit entrepreneur* was an oxymoron. Two such disparate words could hardly coexist. Nonprofits were charitable organizations that worked without profit motive. Indeed, for many, profit was a dirty word. Entrepreneurs, on the other hand, were businessmen for whom profit was both the cardinal reason for existence and the sole definition of success.

In the last decade, and particularly with the advent of the Reagan administration in 1981, the apparent distance between charitable mission and earned income has narrowed. To be sure, nonprofits with money-making ventures have long existed. But these ventures, which include such commercially viable activities as thrift shops, museum stores, university presses, journals and magazines, and sheltered workshops, were more the exception than the rule. The range and size of these entrepreneurial activities, moreover, were generally limited in scope and size.

The incentives to develop enterprise began to be felt in the late 1970s. Reeling from the economic recession and beset by double-digit inflation, nonprofits sought to create ways to finance sharply rising costs. While many worked harder at fund-raising, others began to reach out for more nontraditional funding approaches. One such approach was the creation of a stream of earned income dollars. Put another way, as expenses increased, some nonprofits began to explore both expanding *and* diversifying their sources of revenue.

The Reagan administration heightened the pressure on nonprofits by taking two contradictory positions. First, senior officials relentlessly called for shrinking the size and function of the federal government and turning over the programs to states and localities *(The New Federalism)* and, especially, to the private sector *(privatization)*.

These policies, which increasingly came to look like *load shedding,* began with the idea of selling census data and gold coins. By the middle of the second Reagan administration, they had progressed to include the proposed sale of entire agencies, such as the Federal Housing Administration and the Bonneville Power Authority. Thus, the Reagan administration's first message to nonprofit organizations was to be more entrepreneurial in their activities, and to expand programmatically, especially in areas where the federal government was retreating.

Second, and more immediately decisive, was the negative pressure of increasingly large budget cuts in domestic programs, whose impact was felt heavily by nonprofit organizations. While budget reductions were in full keeping with the principles of load shedding, in reality, without stable or increased funding for domestic programs, the voluntary sector (and, to be sure, the private sector) would be financially unable to pick up the load being shed. To be sure, certain program areas were affected more than others, such as social service organizations, legal and advocacy nonprofits, and environmental groups. (Health services and hospitals, driven by third-party payments, continued to expand.)

Overall, as the eighties progressed, the reality of declining federal support for domestic programs became impossible to ignore, and nonprofit organizations had to search for and find new dollars merely to maintain current activities. Some began to scrutinize their related activities to see where earned income could be maximized.

For some nonprofits, the desire to increase earned revenue had a more positive source of motivation as well. The professionalization of nonprofit management, underway for a decade or more, had produced a cadre of executives more willing and able to act in a businesslike, even entrepreneurial fashion. The Reagan administration's probusiness philosophy coincided with and helped to further legitimize a growing national interest in entrepreneurship. Such interest could hardly be expected to bypass the more capable executives of nonprofit organizations, a number of whom were as alert to business and marketing opportunities as their for-profit counterparts. As a result, some began searching for ways to market existing products or services to new constituencies, while others looked for new products or services to market to current or even new consumer groups.

A final push to increase earned revenue came from the nonprofit environment itself. Here, competition for the limited grant funds of individual, corporate, and foundation donors grew stiffer as federal dollars declined. As the grantsmanship field became more crowded and competitive, the investigation of new, alternative sources of revenue was a logical step.

In sum, the search for earned revenue is the result of several pressures and trends that have been building for at least a decade. The move has not been a sudden, lurching response by the voluntary sector either to apparent commercial opportunity or to draconian budget cuts. Rather, it is the nonprofits' response to a changing environment characterized by tighter budgets, diminishing governmental funds, increased competition for donated dollars, a more receptive national attitude toward enterprise, and the gradual acceptance by some nonprofits that commerce and charity can safely coexist.

A further result of these trends has been the breaking down of traditional service boundaries between the private and voluntary sectors. Whereas before each tended to work in its own ways in its own bailiwick, the boundaries between the two sectors are now increasingly permeable, and each is increasingly willing to contemplate work that once was rejected out of hand.

It should not be assumed that nonprofit enterprise is a universal movement, applicable and pertinent to all organizations at all times. Currently, the numbers of nonprofits engaged in commercial activity is small relative to the entire universe of organizations. The Urban Institute estimates that approximately 15 percent of the nation's 122,000 *nonreligious* nonprofits currently engage in outright sales of products, producing less than 5 percent of their gross revenue. Moreover, for every successful parcel delivery service, home health aide business, or neighborhood supermarket that is successfully developed, many more fail to get off the ground or remain marginal operations. Sadly, no data exist on the number of up-and-running ventures in the country, let alone the ones that are financially successful. While we do know that the interest in and trend toward nonprofit enterprise is growing, the precise trajectory of that growth, and its overall significance to the financial health of the sector, has yet to be plotted.

WHAT IS NONPROFIT ENTERPRISE?

Nonprofit enterprise exists along a spectrum of activity starting with traditional fee-for-service charges and extending into full-scale commercial activity. According to the Urban Institute's Nonprofit Sector Project, approximately 15 percent of nonprofits actually engage in commerce, but more than 70 percent now earn some money through fees and service charges. It is this larger cluster of organizations for whom this book is relevant, since many organizations that charge fees for service commonly operate in a businesslike, market-sensitive manner. They are poised to expand into product or service marketing if they have not already done so. Indeed, examining and updating fee-for-service policies and practices is one starting point for a move into enterprise.

Examples of entrepreneurial activity are plentiful and diverse. They can be categorized according to the product or service being sold in the commercial arena.[1]

Program-Related Products

Nonprofits develop products for sale to organization members, participants, and the public at large. These products are closely identified with the organization on a local or national level. They promote the organization's mission as well as earn money.

Perhaps the best-known example of program-related products are the cookies of the Girl Scouts of America. In this organization, young people learn responsibility while they promulgate the Scouts' mission. In 1986, the Girl Scouts sold 145 million boxes of cookies for gross revenues well in excess of $200 million.

---

[1]This subsection is taken from my "Enterprise and Commerce in Nonprofit Organizations," in *The Nonprofit Sector: A Research Handbook,* ed. Walter W. Powell (New Haven, Ct.: Yale University Press, 1987).

Publishing is an activity to which environmental and cultural organizations have long been attracted. Sierra Club calendars and books, for example, detail the natural beauty of the environment and sell well. Other conservation organizations, like the National Geographic Society and the Museum of National History, publish widely read magazines. In 1982, *National Geographic* grossed $22 million in (taxable) advertising revenue in addition to its $152 million in (untaxable) subscription and membership revenues.

Health-related nonprofits sell products too. For a time, the Planned Parenthood® Federation of America sold its own "house-brand" condom to its affiliates and clinics. The American Red Cross (and many local blood centers) sell fractionated blood products commercially and for research and recently introduced a first-aid "pillow."

Across the nation a wide range of program-related products is sold by a diverse group of organizations. Products range from wearable goods associated with "A Prairie Home Companion" radio program, sold through mail order catalogs by Minnesota Public Radio, to a book on how to choose a nursing home by FRIA, a small consumer-activist organization based in New York City.

Program-Related Services

Nonprofits provide ancillary commercial services to members, friends, and alumni, which enhance the tax exempt mission of the organization. The services may be available to the general public as well. Some services are run by the organization, while others are leased to concessionaires, generally for a percentage of gross revenue.

A typical program-related service is the gift shop commonly found in cultural institutions and hospitals. Perhaps the best known of these shops is run by the Metropolitan Museum of Art, whose overall merchandise and publication revenues exceeded $40 million in 1986. Some of these shops are run largely or entirely by volunteers. The New York City Ballet Gift Bar is one such enterprise. It is open one-half hour before dance programs and during program intermissions. Gross revenues of the Gift Bar exceed $125,000 annually; the net to the City Ballet is roughly half that amount. Parking lots are another source of revenue. Clients and patrons need places to park near the facility they are visiting, and they are willing to pay for the service.

Another area is food sales—even self-service vending machines. Cultural institutions, hospitals, and educational institutions run restaurants or cafeterias for the convenience of relatives visiting a patient, for patrons at an exhibition, or for ticketholders during the intermission of a concert or play. For example, the Smithsonian Institution in Washington, D.C., grosses more than $11 million in food and beverage sales annually.

There are many other related services. For example, organizing tours and travel packages for the members, students, faculty, and graduates of educational and cultural organizations are now commonplace activities. The Museum of Natural History and the American Jewish Congress are especially well known for the tour programs they sponsor.

Staff and Client Resources

Nonprofit organizations provide the expertise of their staff members and clients in a variety of commercial ventures. These ventures may offer similar services to new groups of consumers; new, related services to current consumers; or, perhaps, both.

As an example in the arts, the Guthrie Theatre in Minneapolis has offered its computerized box office system and the assistance to set it up to other nonprofit theatres. WNET-13, the New York PBS television station, provides its production and post-production services to corporate and nonprofit clients. The Spence School in New York provides computer support to a dozen other private schools in Manhattan. Librarians consult on book preservation and collection management.

Numerous social service organizations have consulted for the private sector in designing alcoholism and drug treatment programs, and some are now designing comprehensive employee assistance programs as well. Family Service America, a national nonprofit, provides drug and alcohol counseling abuse programs for all General Motors employees, retirees, and their families. The Miami Valley Hospital in Dayton, Ohio, offers financial and management consulting services to other hospitals in the local area.

Possibly the most lucrative area to develop in recent years is the long-term research contract between private corporations (the contractor) and universities. It is also one of the most problem-ridden areas. These contracts often involve large amounts of money. They raise such issues as the dedication of staff time to commercial products, the use of tax exempt university facilities for profit-making clients, academic freedom, the integrity of basic research, and the ownership and control of patents. Harvard, Stanford, and Washington University in St. Louis have contemplated or signed long-term contracts with sponsoring corporations, and agreements involving several other universities and corporations are in the offing.

Some social service nonprofits also employ their own clients in commercial activities. These ventures are most commonly conducted in sheltered workshops operating through federal or state contracts, under strict regulation. Due to their large social service and training components, few ventures earn much profit, although the sheltered workshop operations of Goodwill Industries, the Salvation Army, and the Volunteers of America are among the financially strongest.

"Hard Property"

The sale, lease, development, and rental of land and buildings is an increasingly common area of earned income. Much of the income derives from making use of facility down-time, i.e., fixed resources that lie idle during some part of the day.

For example, many schools and colleges rent excess dormitory and cafeteria space during slack summer months to special conventions or traveling adult education programs. Some private schools and universities lease their stadia to professional sports teams for training and practice, while others use their tennis courts for tennis camps and ice rinks for community or private leagues. Renting auditoriums, kitchen facilities, and even equipment is increasingly common. National Public Radio even leases transponders on its satellite during its broadcast downtime.

The Rensselaer Polytechnic Institute in Troy, New York, has taken the concept further. It has set aside campus facilities to "incubate" high technology industry and encourage successful ventures to stay in the local area. It charges a low rent for the facilities.

In another "hard property" area, the National Audubon Society has for decades leased sections of its Rainey Bird Sanctuary in Louisiana for mineral exploration, under tightly controlled agreements. Universities in the western part of the United States lease land to ranchers and farmers for grazing and irrigation.

The sale of air rights is a notable, if infrequent, occurrence. In the 1970s, the Museum of Modern Art sold the air rights over its building for $17 million plus substantial annual payments to a tax exempt trust created by state legislation. More recently, sale–leaseback transactions involving land and buildings of the Oakland Museum and Bennington College have been arranged. These sale–leaseback transactions by nonprofit organizations were sharply curtailed by Congress in the Tax Reform Act of 1984.

Finally, some organizations expand into new space more than sufficient for their needs and lease out the excess. For example, the Municipal Arts Society of New York City purchased the North Wing of the landmark Villard Houses in Manhattan. It receives commercial rents from the lease of two floors of the building and uses the money to subsidize its own operating costs on the remaining floors.

"Soft Property"

Soft property encompasses a cluster of income-earning assets that include copyrights, patents, trademarks, art and artifacts, and even mailing and membership lists.

Two especially active organizations in licensing products for royalty payments are Children's Television Workshop and the National Wildlife Federation. CTW licenses its "Sesame Street" characters for adaptation in books, toys, records, and soft products to for-profit commercial firms. In 1982, the organization grossed $9 million in royalties from its agreements. Similarly, the Federation licenses its well-known Ranger Rick character. On a different front, the Bank Street College of Education recently developed the Bank Street Writer, a piece of word-processing software now licensed for sale to two firms dealing in the commercial and educational marketplace.

Some organizations permit their names to be used by, and often contribute to, commercial publications of high quality, which are related to their own activities. One such group is the National Audubon Society, which licenses its name for the Audubon and Peterson Field Guides, as well as for the Audubon Elephant Folio, published in limited reproductions. Commercially attractive products are also reproduced from collections of art, artifacts, and furniture. For example, Winterthur and the Museum of the City of New York license reproductions of period-piece furniture. The Metropolitan Museum of Art has earned substantial income by licensing artistic designs from its collections to textile companies. Finally, many nonprofits increase revenues by renting membership and mailing lists to other nonprofits, and even to commercial firms.

WHAT ARE THE BENEFITS OF ENTERPRISE?

Nonprofits willing and able to earn a portion of their income can benefit in several ways. First and most basic is the ability to increase the organization's income, in order to return the profits to program activities. In some cases the revenue stream will be substantial; in others it will be small relative to the operating budget of the organization. In either case, if the cost to the organization is less than the attendant benefits, then the net of the venture will be positive.

A second financial advantage is the enhancement of the organizations' health. Earned income helps to diversify their revenue base, providing a cushion against changes in the funding or contracting climate. Indeed, changes in governmental funding may lead to corresponding shifts in corporate or foundation funding, whose priorities may be altered in order to deal with the consequences of governmental withdrawal. To the degree that nonprofits can diversify their revenue streams, they can insulate themselves from the consequences of changed policies.

Nonprofits that pursue earned income activities often improve their management capabilities as well. Business demands constant, concerted attention to bottom line considerations. Policy choices of nonprofits become informed by dollar considerations, which, when prudently introduced, often improve the quality of decision-making. Moreover, new staff may be hired to attend to the commercial aspects of the organization, and the businesslike approach can rub off on other employees. Further, management information systems are often created or upgraded. Experience has shown that when management spends more time on the financial consequences of its activities, it is generally more rigorous and realistic when making programmatic decisions as well. Thus, the introduction of enterprise brings with it a new mindset within the organization—one that is more calculating and skilled in directing the course of the agency.

A further, related benefit is the introduction of new financial discipline within the organization. For example, the creation or expansion of enterprise may involve borrowing funds or selling equity to an investor. The reporting requirements of lenders or investors often usher in a new vigilance on the part of nonprofit executives. Decisions are made with better information, and may happen more quickly than previously. Even though the organization may not always appreciate dealing with bankers or investors (or suppliers), expansion into the market economy often leads to an enhanced management capacity.

Another positive result, in general, occurs in the area of fund-raising. Foundations and corporations are increasingly pressing their grantees to find ways to pay for programs that have a limited funding life. If earned income can be used to at least partially replace charitable dollars, funders will be more responsive to funding requests from nonprofit organizations. Individual contributors also appear to respond favorably to nonprofit enterprise. Success in enterprise, particularly in a well publicized area, seems to imply that the organization is successful in all its service areas. Whether or not this is always true, funders, both individual and institutional, like "winners." Anecdotal evidence supports the view that organizations with a successful earned income component have enhanced their appeal to foundations and corporations.

Earned income can also strengthen the organization at the board level by attracting new board members with skills and energy to devote to both enterprise and the nonprofit cause. This can reinvigorate a board. Further, the broadening of board membership can also mean new contacts in funding circles.

Finally, successful earned income ventures can increase the visibility of the organization undertaking them. In the highly competitive world of grantsmanship, good press can translate into increased financial support by enabling the organization to present its case in an appealing way and in a variety of forums.

To be sure, earned income activities present pitfalls as well. When poorly planned or executed, they can endanger the financial and program stability of the nonprofit, distract it from its exempt mission, engender destructive competition for scarce resources, hurt staff morale, and hinder fund-raising efforts. Thus, nonprofits must enter the entrepreneurial arena well prepared for serious, hard, and relentless activity. Enterprise, even under the best circumstances, is a difficult endeavor. Those who begin in an unprepared or blithe manner are bound to fail.

In the chapters that follow, the authors take a prudent, measured approach to nonprofit enterprise. Each writes from the perspective of both practitioner and advisor. Bruce Hopkins provides an essential overview of the legal issues involved in both nonprofit status in general and earned income venturing in particular. Edward Skloot's two chapters are a basic "starter kit" for new ventures, although those groups with ongoing ventures will find in them several useful ideas and approaches as well.

The chapter by Christopher Lovelock and Charles Weinberg takes a longer look at marketing, stressing both the uniqueness of nonprofit organizations and the universality of good marketing techniques. Cynthia Massarsky's essay on business planning deliberately uses a "hybrid case," i.e., a nonprofit organization with multiple agendas— doing good and earning income at the same time. Ellen Arrick focuses on financial questions and illuminates for the reader how the investor or lender views risk and draws up risk profiles. The chapter by Wim Wiewel pays particular attention to structural issues and the decision points that organizations must pass through to get the form of their venture right.

The last two chapters discuss venturing from the vantage point of a specific subsector of the nonprofit world. The first, by Elliott Lang, focuses on museums and their shop operations. The second, by Nancy Haycock, speaks to the pitfalls of venturing and focuses directly on smaller nonprofits. She describes specific cases that illuminate the problems. Both caution that every step of the way must be taken with prudence and an eye to lowering risk.

If one message underpins this book, it is that there is no substitute for good analysis and ongoing vigilance. Like any difficult activity, venturing has its rules of success. The more one learns them and sticks by them, the greater the likelihood that the venturing will provide a rewarding experience.

While this book was in the later stages of preparation the issue of competition between the voluntary and the private sectors began to take on increasing currency. For example, in the summer of 1987 the Oversight Subcommittee of the House Ways and Means Committee held hearings on the unrelated business income tax and on inter-sectoral competition. As of the late summer these concerns have become prominent in discussions of nonprofit enterprise.

Still, it is not clear what the long-term effect of "the competition issue" will be. I have chosen to avoid discussion that would be dated or only partially relevant. What follows is still entirely pertinent to the concerns of nonprofit executives, board members, and other interested persons.

1

The Legal Context of Nonprofit Enterprise

BRUCE R. HOPKINS

THE PURPOSE OF THIS ANALYSIS is to describe the context in law in which nonprofit enterprise is started and operates. For many, the words nonprofit and enterprise do not mesh well conceptually.

However, the term nonprofit does not mean no profit. Instead, the concept of a nonprofit organization essentially focuses on the disposition of the profits that are generated.

Thus, the words nonprofit and enterprise do not harbor a conflict; they are quite compatible under the existing federal tax law structure. Those who assert them to be incompatible lack an understanding of the legal meaning of the term nonprofit organization.

A summary of the legal context in which enterprises by nonprofit organizations are created and flourish requires a brief discussion of both the legal meaning of the term nonprofit organization and the tax exemption requirements. This discussion follows, along with a summary of the unrelated income rules and some advice as to effective use of these and other federal tax law opportunities.

MEANING OF THE TERM NONPROFIT

A nonprofit organization is an organization such as a corporation or trust that is organized and operated for a purpose other than the economic advancement of those who provide its capital. In many instances, a nonprofit organization is a tax-exempt organization, such as a charitable or educational entity.

As noted, despite frequent misconceptions, the concept of a nonprofit organization does not mean an organization that cannot enjoy a profit. (For our purposes, the term profit means an excess of revenue over expenses.) Rather, the term means that a nonprofit organization's profit may not be distributed to persons in their private capacities.

The basic distinction between a nonprofit organization and a for-profit one is that the latter has owners. These owners are the holders of the equity in the business. If the business entity is a corporation, the owners are the shareholders; if it is a partnership, the owners are the partners. The purpose of the business is to generate a profit for its owners. In the case of corporations, for example, the profits are passed to the owners (shareholders) in the form of dividends.

Thus, the term for-profit means that some or all of the profits generated by the business activity are passed along to the equity owners. The term has nothing to do with the organization producing a profit for its use in program and administration. Nonprofit organizations can generate profits at the entity level, but cannot pass profits along to persons as equity owners. That is why the federal tax law states that, in the case of some nonprofit organizations, the organization's net earnings may not inure to the benefit of persons in their private capacity.

MEANING OF TAX EXEMPTION

The terms nonprofit organization and tax-exempt organization are not synonymous. The concept of the nonprofit organization is broader than that of the tax-exempt organization.

Basically, the law as to nonprofit organizations is state law, while the law as to tax-exempt organizations essentially is federal law. Not all nonprofit organizations are tax-exempt, although an organization must be a nonprofit entity to be a tax-exempt entity. Fundamentally, the matter comes down to this: an organization must first qualify under state law as a nonprofit organization to thereafter qualify under federal law as a tax-exempt organization. There are, of course, many categories of tax-exempt organizations (ranging from charities and membership associations to political committees and cooperatives), and many are entitled to state-law tax exemptions once federal tax-exempt status is received.

A tax-exempt organization thus means an organization that is relieved from the obligation to pay one or more taxes. While all of these entities are nonprofit, they are not necessarily exempt from all taxes and certainly not exempt from requirements of law outside the tax context (such as the labor, antigambling, or, in some instances, antitrust laws).

Tax-exempt status is a matter of law, with eligibility for federal tax exemption a subject of the Internal Revenue Code. Therefore, the Internal Revenue Service does not grant tax exemption but rather grants recognition of tax-exempt status.

FEDERAL TAX REQUIREMENTS

To be a tax-exempt organization under federal law, an organization must satisfy an *organizational test* and an *operational test*. These tests are more articulated in the case of charitable organizations.[1] However, they are essentially applicable with respect to all categories of tax-exempt entities.

The organizational test looks to the nature of the organization's governing documents. The federal tax law assumes that a tax-exempt organization will have two documents in this regard: a document that creates the entity and one that provides its basic rules of operation. The former document is termed the *articles of organization*.

There are basically three types of tax-exempt organization: the nonprofit corporation, the trust, and the unincorporated association. The articles of organization for these three entities are, respectively, the articles of incorporation, the declaration of trust (or trust agreement), or constitution. For most tax-exempt organizations, the document that states its basic rules of organization are its bylaws.

The requirements of the organizational test must be satisfied by language in the organization's articles of organization. It is not sufficient to merely reflect these requirements in a collateral document, such as bylaws.

The organizational test principally requires, in the case of charitable organizations, that upon dissolution or liquidation the net income and assets of the organization be distributed to one or more other qualified charitable organizations. The test also requires that the organization's statement of purposes be in conformance with its tax-exempt status.

The operational test looks to determine whether an organization's actual operations are in conformance with the requirements of the particular tax-exempt classification. In the case of charitable organizations, the test assesses whether, for example, net earnings are flowing to persons in their private capacity, too much lobbying is occurring, and/or political campaign activities are taking place.

Some activities (such as political campaign activities by a charitable organization) go to the heart of an organization's tax-exempt status. Others are less critical but nonetheless significant. The best illustration of the latter is the conduct of *unrelated activities,* which, while they may trigger a tax liability, do not necessarily deprive an organization of its federal tax exemption.

In the normal course of events, a tax-exempt organization will not contravene the organizational test. This is because the organization's governing instruments are properly prepared or, if not, were revised as the result of the adverse reaction of the IRS during the process of securing recognition of tax exemption. A common violation of the organizational test, however, is the failure of the articles of organization of a charitable organization to contain the requisite dissolution clause.

By contrast, the operational test relates to the entirety of an organization's ongoing operations. In the case of a charitable organization, for example, the test is violated where the organization is not operated principally for tax-exempt purposes, allows its net earnings to inure to individuals in their private capacities, engages in a substantial amount of legislative activities, participates or intervenes in a political campaign, or operates one or more unrelated businesses to an impermissible extent.

---

1. That is, organizations described in Internal Revenue Code of 1986 section ("IRC §") 501(c)(3) and exempt from federal income taxation under IRC §501(a).

Essentially, the operational test for charitable organizations is intended to assure that the organization is functioning in the public interest, rather than in advancement of private ends.

THE UNRELATED INCOME RULES

The treatment of unrelated activities represents the most dynamic and controversial aspect of federal tax law facing tax-exempt organizations today. Although the rules were enacted in 1950, it was not until the early 1970s that this body of tax law emerged as the most important to tax-exempt organizations.

The unrelated income rules were significantly rewritten in 1969. This was done to add to the statutory law many of the basic principles that the Department of the Treasury and the IRS had attempted to impose by regulation—attempts that were voided by the courts. The revisions in 1969 brought about a statutory definition of the term *trade or business,* the *fragmentation rule* (see below), and an array of other refinements and expansions of the rules.

The original concept underlying these rules was that of the *outside* business owned and operated by a tax-exempt organization. That is, the unrelated business rules were initially written on the assumption that the unrelated business owned and operated by a tax-exempt organization is in a separate organization, rather than operated as an activity within the tax-exempt organization. However, Congress significantly expanded the reach of the rules by authorizing the IRS to evaluate activities conducted by tax-exempt organizations themselves.

This law change reflected the fact that most tax-exempt organizations that engage in unrelated business activity do so as part of the range of activities of the organization itself. For example, a charitable organization may publish a journal as an exempt function, yet sell advertising in the journal; the sale of advertising is an unrelated activity, separate from the general publishing activity. Likewise, a museum may as an exempt function operate a gift shop that is reflective of its collection, yet be taxable on the sale of souvenirs to the general public. Similar is a hospital that may without taxation operate a pharmacy for the benefit of its patients, yet be taxable on the sale of pharmaceuticals to the general public.

The objective of the unrelated business income tax is to prevent unfair competition between tax-exempt organizations and for-profit, commercial enterprises.[2] Prior to the enactment of these rules, a tax-exempt organization could operate a for-profit business and undercut the for-profit competition by charging lower prices, which was made possible because the tax-exempt organization, in determining price levels, did not have to take taxes and the inurement of profits to shareholders into account. The rules are intended to place the unrelated business activities of an exempt organization on the same tax footing as the nonexempt business with which it competes.

---

2. Reg. §1.513-1(b).

Prior to enactment of the unrelated income rules in 1950, the law embodied the so-called destination of income test.[3] Pursuant to this standard, the law merely required that the net profits of tax-exempt organizations be used in furtherance of their exempt purposes. The test did not consider the source of the profits, thereby tolerating forms of unfair competition. Under this approach, a for-profit business could be a tax-exempt organization simply by paying over its net profits to charity.

In summary, in adopting these rules in 1950 and in making them more stringent in 1969, Congress did not prohibit commercial ventures by nonprofit organizations, nor did it levy taxes only on the net receipts of businesses that bear no relation at all to the tax-exempt purposes of nonprofit organizations. Instead, it struck a balance, as the United States Supreme Court later phrased it, between "its two objectives of encouraging benevolent enterprise and restraining unfair competition."[4]

Affected Tax-Exempt Organizations

Nearly all types of tax-exempt organizations are subject to the unrelated income rules. They include charitable entities, scientific entities, religious organizations (including churches), educational organizations (including schools, colleges, and universities), health care organizations (including hospitals), social welfare organizations, labor organizations (including unions), trade and professional associations, and veterans' groups.

Special rules tax the income not related to exempt functions of social clubs, homeowners' associations, and political organizations.

Certain organizations are not generally subject to the unrelated income rules, simply because they are not allowed to engage in active business endeavors, such as private foundations and title-holding corporations.

The unrelated income rules are applicable to all organizations that are tax-exempt,[5] other than instrumentalities of the United States.[6]

Loss of Exemption

To be tax-exempt, an organization must be organized and operated primarily for exempt purposes.[7] The federal tax law, however, allows an exempt organization to engage in a certain amount of activity unrelated to its exempt purposes.[8] Nonetheless, there is no fixed percentage or other mechanical test for determining whether an unrelated activity or amount of unrelated income will deprive an organization of its tax exemption.

A reasonable guideline in this regard is a 20 percent standard. If a tax-exempt organization is engaging in unrelated activities or receiving unrelated income in excess

---

3. Trinidad v. Sagrada Orden de Predicatores, 263 U.S. 578 (1924).
4. United States v. American College of Physicians, 106 S.Ct. 1591 U.S. (1986).
5. That is, are tax-exempt under IRC §501(a) as being described in IRC §501(c).
6. IRC §511(a)(2)(A).
7. Better Business Bureau of Washington, D.C. v. United States, 326 U.S. 279 (1945).
8. For example, in the case of charitable organizations, Reg. §1.501(c)(3)-1(e)(1).

of that threshold, the situation should be carefully evaluated. While transgression of this standard is by no means automatically indicative of impending revocation of tax exemption, it should be grounds for continuing scrutiny.

When an organization derives net income from one or more unrelated business activities, known as *unrelated business taxable income,* it is subject to tax on that income. An organization's exemption will be revoked if an inappropriate portion of its activities is not in furtherance of an exempt purpose.[9]

Business activities may preclude initial qualification of an otherwise tax-exempt organization as a charitable or other entity. This would occur because it would fail to satisfy the operational test, which, as noted, looks to see whether the organization is being operated principally for exempt purposes. Likewise, an organization will not meet the organizational test if its articles of organization empower it, as more than an insubstantial part of its activities, to carry on activities that are not in furtherance of its exempt purpose.

An organization may satisfy the operational test even when it operates a trade or business as a substantial part of its activities. As long as the trade or business is in furtherance of the organization's exempt purpose, and it is not operated for the primary purpose of carrying on an unrelated trade or business, considerable amounts of money can be earned.[10]

It is because of this rule that, without loss of tax exemption, schools, colleges, and universities can operate dormitories, cafeterias, and bookstores; hospitals can operate gift shops, snack bars, and parking lots; museums can operate gift shops and catalog-sales programs; and theaters, orchestras, and operas can charge for performances.

If the organization's primary purpose for carrying on a trade or business is for profit, however, it is expressly denied exemption on the ground that it constitutes a *feeder organization.*[11] This is notwithstanding the fact that all of its profits are payable to one or more tax-exempt organizations.

THE THREE UNRELATED INCOME TESTS

In application of the unrelated income rules, there are essentially three tests: 1) is the activity a trade or business, 2) is it regularly carried on, and 3) is the activity related to the tax-exempt organizations's program purposes?[12]

Concept of *Trade or Business*

For purposes of the federal tax rules, the term *trade or business* includes "any activity which is carried on for the production of income from the sale of goods or the performance of services."[13]

---

9. For example, in the case of charitable organizations, Reg. §1.501(c)(3)-1(c)(1).
10. Reg. §1.501(c)(3)-1(c)(1).
11. IRC §502.
12. Reg. §1.513-1(a).
13. IRC §513(c).

Accordingly, most activities that would constitute a trade or business under basic tax law principles[14] are considered a trade or business for purposes of the unrelated income rules.[15]

This definition of trade or business is very encompassing and embraces nearly every activity of a tax-exempt organization. Absent a specific statutory exemption (see below), only investment activities generally escape this classification.

Consequently, every tax-exempt organization is viewed, under the federal tax law, as a bundle of activities, each of which (other than investment functions) is a *business*.

The IRS is empowered to examine each of the activities in the bundle in search of unrelated business endeavor. This is known as the *fragmentation rule*. As Congress chose to state the principle, "An activity does not lose identity as a trade or business merely because it is carried on within a larger aggregate of similar activities or within a larger complex of other endeavors which may, or may not, be related to the exempt purposes of the organization."[16]

The fragmentation rule (which, as noted, was grafted onto the unrelated business income rules in 1969) is at the heart of the contemporary application of these rules. Empowered by this rule, the IRS can examine each activity of an organization in the bundle, in isolation from the others.

The fragmentation rule allows the IRS to differentiate between the exempt function of an educational organization in publishing a journal and the taxable activity of selling advertising in the journal, the exempt function of a college in selling books and the nonexempt function of selling appliances, the exempt function of a hospital in selling pharmaceuticals to its patients but not to the general public, the exempt function of a museum in selling items reflective of its collection but not souvenirs of the city in which it is located, and the exempt function of an association in providing dues-funded services to its members but not in making insurance available to its members.

The IRS can delve into great detail in application of the fragmentation rule. An example is the case of the tax-exempt blood bank that sells blood plasma to commercial laboratories but also maintains inventories of blood and blood products that are furnished to hospitals for patient use. The fragmentation rule was applied to allow the blood bank to engage in the related activity of selling by-product plasma (whole blood less red blood cells), yet the activity of selling plasmapheresed plasma (where the red cells are separated and replaced in the blood donors, and the resulting plasma collected) was ruled to be an unrelated activity because this plasma is not a product resulting from the performance of the bank's tax-exempt functions.[17]

Congress also enacted a law that states, "[w]here an activity carried on for profit constitutes an unrelated trade or business, no part of such trade or business shall be excluded from such classification merely because it does not result in profit."[18] This

14. IRC §162.
15. Reg. §1.513-1(b).
16. IRC §513(c).
17. Rev. Rul. 78-145, 1978-1 C.B. 169.
18. IRC §513(c).

rule prevents an activity from losing its status as an unrelated activity simply because it fails in a particular year to in fact generate more revenue than allocable expenses.

Concept of *Regularly Carried On*

To be considered an unrelated business, an activity of a tax-exempt organization must be "regularly carried on by it."[19]

Income from an activity is considered taxable only when, assuming the other criteria are satisfied, the activity is regularly carried on, as distinguished from sporadic or infrequent activity.[20] The factors that determine whether an activity is regularly carried on are, in the language of the tax regulations, the *frequency* and *continuity* of the activities, and the *manner* in which the activities are pursued.[21] In essence, this test looks to determine whether the acts, although a business, are being actively conducted in a *commercial* manner.

These factors must be evaluated in light of the purpose of the unrelated business income tax, which, as noted, is to place tax-exempt organizations' unrelated business activities upon the same tax basis as their nonexempt business competitors. Thus, specific business activities of a tax-exempt organization will generally "be deemed . . . 'regularly carried on' if they manifest a frequency and continuity, and are pursued in a manner generally similar to comparable commercial activities of nonexempt organizations."[22]

Where income-producing activities are performed by for-profit organizations on a year-round basis, the performance of the activities for a period of only a few weeks by a tax-exempt organization generally does not constitute the regular carrying on of a trade or business.[23] For example, a sandwich stand operated by a hospital auxiliary for two weeks at a state fair does not constitute the regular conduct of business.[24] Likewise, a variety of fund-raising activities, such as the occasional dance, theater party, or auction, escape taxation under this rule.

Similarly, occasional or annual income-producing activities, such as fund-raising events, do not constitute a business that is regularly carried on. However, the conduct of year-round business activities, such as a parking lot rental, for one day each week constitutes the regular carrying on of a business.[25] Where commercial entities normally undertake income-producing activities on a seasonal basis, the conduct of the activities by an exempt organization during a significant portion of the season is deemed the regular conduct of the activity.[26] Thus, the marketing of Christmas cards during that holiday season is measured by the duration of that season, just as the operation of a horse-racing track is measured in terms of the racing season.

19. IRC §512(a)(1).
20. Reg. §1.513-1(c).
21. Reg. §1.513-1(c)(1).
22. *Ibid.*
23. Reg. §1.513-1(c)(2)(i).
24. *Ibid.*
25. Reg. §1.513-1(c)(2)(i).
26. *Ibid.*

A trade or business is regularly carried on if the attributes of the activity are similar to the commercial activities of nonexempt organizations.[27]

Concept of *Unrelated Trade or Business*

The term *unrelated trade or business* is defined to mean "any trade or business the conduct of which is not substantially related (aside from the need of such organization for income or funds or the use it makes of the profits derived) to the exercise or performance by such organization of its charitable, educational, or other purpose or function constituting the basis for its exemption."[28] Thus, the need of an organization for the income derived from an activity does not make the activity a related one.

A trade or business regularly conducted by a nonprofit organization is subject to tax, unless it is substantially related to the accomplishment of the exempt purpose of the organization.[29] To be substantially related, the activity must have a substantial *causal relationship* to the achievement of an exempt purpose.[30]

The fact that an asset is essential to the conduct of an organization's exempt activities does not shield income of the organization from taxation where the income was produced by that asset in a way that is unrelated to the exempt purposes.[31] The income-producing activities must still meet the causal relationship test if the income is not to be subject to tax.[32] This issue arises when an organization owns a facility or other assets that are put to a dual use. For example, the operation of an auditorium as a motion-picture theater for public entertainment in the evening would be treated as an unrelated activity even though the theater is used exclusively for exempt purposes during regular hours.[33] Likewise, a tax-exempt organization may sell excess time on its computer, with that sales activity constituting an unrelated business. (As discussed below, some activities may be structured as rental arrangements, where the income is nontaxable as *passive* income.)

A related concept is that activities should not be conducted on a scale larger than is reasonably necessary for the performance of the exempt functions.[34] Activities in excess of the needs of exempt functions constitute the conduct of an unrelated business.[35] Thus, a retail grocery store operation, formed to sell food in a poverty area at lower-than-usual prices and to provide job training for unemployed residents of the area, was found to not qualify for tax exemption because the operation was conducted on a much larger scale than reasonably necessary for the training program.[36]

27. Reg. §1.513-1(c).
28. IRC §513(a).
29. Reg. §1.513-1(a).
30. Reg. §1.513-1(d)(2).
31. Reg. §1.513-1(d).
32. Reg. §1.513-1(d)(2).
33. *Ibid.*
34. Reg. §1.513-1(d)(3).
35. *Ibid.*
36. Rev. Rul. 73-127, 1973-1 C.B. 221.

DEFINITION OF UNRELATED BUSINESS TAXABLE INCOME

As noted, to be subject to the unrelated income rules, an income-earning activity must satisfy three tests. These tests, then, are built into the definition of the term *unrelated business taxable income.*

That term is defined as "the gross income derived by any organization from any unrelated trade or business . . . regularly carried on by it, less the deductions allowed . . . [under federal tax law] which are directly connected with the carrying on of such trade or business."[37]

Both this gross income and allowable deductions are computed in conformance with the modifications described below.

If a trade or business regularly carried on by a partnership in which a tax-exempt organization is a member is an unrelated trade or business with respect to the organization, the organization, in computing its unrelated business taxable income, must (subject to the modifications) include its share (whether or not distributed) of the gross income of the partnership from the unrelated business and its share of the partnership deductions directly connected with the gross income.[38] The purpose of this rule is to prevent a tax-exempt organization from avoiding the unrelated business income tax by conducting an unrelated business within a partnership.

Tax-exempt organizations are subject to tax on their unrelated business taxable income at ordinary corporate rates or at the individual rates if the organization is not incorporated.[39] For tax years beginning on or after July 1, 1987, the taxable income of corporations of $50,000 or less is taxed at a rate of 15 percent; a 25-percent rate applies to corporate income of $50,000 to $75,000; and a 34-percent rate applies to corporate income over $75,000. For years beginning after December 31, 1986, tax-exempt organizations must make quarterly estimated payments of the tax on unrelated business income, under the same rules that require payments of corporate income taxes.

EXEMPTED ACTIVITIES

Despite the foregoing general rules, certain businesses conducted by tax-exempt organizations are expressly exempted from taxation.

Exempted from taxation is a trade or business "in which substantially all the work in carrying on such trade or business is performed for the organization without compensation."[40] This exemption protects from taxation many ongoing charitable fund-raising activities.

Also exempted is a trade or business that is carried on by the organization "primarily for the convenience of its members, students, patients, officers, or employees."[41] This

37. IRC §512(a)(1).
38. IRC §512(c).
39. IRC §511(a), (b).
40. IRC §513(a)(1).
41. IRC §513(a)(2).

exception is available to organizations that are charitable, educational, and the like,[42] or are governmental colleges and universities,[43] as contrasted with other categories of tax-exempt organizations. Many of the sales of college and university bookstores, for example, are exempt from taxation by virtue of this rule.

Further exempted is a trade or business "which is the selling of merchandise, substantially all of which has been received by the organization as gifts or contributions."[44] This exemption shelters the work of exempt thrift stores from taxation.

The term *unrelated trade or business* does not include "qualified public entertainment activities."[45] These activities are usually conducted at fairs or expositions promoting agricultural and educational purposes.

The term unrelated trade or business also does not include "qualified convention and trade show activities."[46] The purpose of these activities usually is to attract persons in an industry generally (without regard to membership in the sponsoring organization), as well as members of the public, to the show. Reasons to draw visitors include displaying industry products or to stimulate interest in, and demand for, industry products or services, or to educate persons engaged in the industry in the development of new products and services or new rules and regulations affecting the industry.

For a tax-exempt hospital, the concept of unrelated trade or business does not include the furnishing of certain services to one or more other tax-exempt hospitals under certain circumstances.[47] The concept of unrelated trade or business also does not include any trade or business that consists of conducting bingo games.[48]

EXEMPTED INCOME

Certain types of income are exempt from the unrelated income tax.

Because the unrelated income tax applies to active businesses conducted by tax-exempt organizations, most types of passive income are exempt from taxation. This exemption generally covers dividends, interest, payments with respect to securities, loans, annuities, royalties, most rents, capital gains, and gains on the lapse or termination of options written by the organization.[49] Many exempt organizations are able to escape the tax on unrelated business activity by empowering another party (usually by license) to act on its behalf in the operation of a business, with compensation to the exempt organization set as a function of an objective criterion, such as the volume of sales (and thus as a royalty). For example, an exempt organization may be compensated in an amount equal to a set percentage of the value of an item sold by a business pursuant to contract with the business; if the exempt

42. That is, are described in IRC §501(c)(3).
43. That is, are described in IRC §511(a)(2)(B).
44. IRC §513(a)(3).
45. IRC §513(d).
46. IRC §513(d).
47. IRC §513(e).
48. IRC §513(f).
49. IRC §512(b)(1), (2), (3), and (5).

organization is not involved in the marketing of the item, the compensation generally will not be taxable.

However, the unrelated debt-financed income rules override the general exemption for passive income.[50] These rules generally cause receipt of some taxable income, even where the income is derived passively, where the income can be traced to a borrowing by the tax-exempt organization.

Also, interest, annuities, royalties, and rents derived from a controlled corporation may be taxable.[51] (For this purpose, the term *control* means ownership of at least 80 percent of the stock, directly or indirectly.) This rule prevents a tax-exempt organization from skirting the unrelated income tax by operating one or more unrelated businesses in a subsidiary and deriving income from the subsidiary (which takes a deduction for the payments) as a form of passive revenue. However, a tax-exempt organization may receive tax-free dividends from a controlled subsidiary (with no deduction in the subsidiary for the payments). Thus, a tax-exempt organization may operate a controlled subsidiary, yet pay tax on income received from it in the form of rent, interest, or royalties.

There are three exemptions pertaining to the conduct of research. Income derived from research for the United States, or any of its agencies or instrumentalities, or any state or political subdivision thereof, is exempted from taxation.[52] In the case of a college, university, or hospital, income derived from research performed for any person is exempted.[53] In the case of an organization operated primarily for purposes of carrying on fundamental research, the results of which are freely available to the general public, income derived from research performed for any person is exempted.[54]

There is a specific deduction of $1,000.[55] This enables a tax-exempt organization to receive, without taxation, up to $1,000 in unrelated income annually.

Reporting Requirements

A tax-exempt organization experiencing unrelated taxable income must file a tax return for the year(s) involved with the IRS.[56] This return is on Form 990-T. Income that is derived passively is investment income and is reported on the tax-exempt organization's annual information return (usually Form 990).

A tax-exempt organization can have more than one unrelated business. An unrelated business can operate at a loss. Thus, in computing unrelated income for a year, a tax-exempt organization can net the gains of profitable unrelated business with the losses of unprofitable unrelated businesses to arrive at any net unrelated income for the year. Any such net income is, as noted, further reduced by a specific deduction.

50. IRC §512(b)(4) and 514.
51. IRC §512(b)(13).
52. IRC §512(b)(7).
53. IRC §512(b)(8).
54. IRC §512(b)(9).
55. IRC §512(b)(12).
56. IRC §6012.

USE OF SUBSIDIARIES

Some tax-exempt organizations are electing to "spin off" their unrelated activities to related taxable subsidiaries, so that the tax on the net income of the unrelated activity will not be borne by the exempt organization.

This can happen where the managers of the tax-exempt organization are averse to reporting any unrelated income, for fear of negative perceptions of the organization or that such income will encourage an IRS audit, or where the unrelated activity is too large in relation to related activity.

As long as the subsidiary is created for true business activities, the law regards the tax-exempt parent and the for-profit subsidiary as separate legal entities.[57] This means that when the subsidiary is organized with the bona fide intention that it will have some real and substantial business function, its existence will not be disregarded for tax purposes.[58] However, where the parent corporation so controls the affairs of the subsidiary that it is merely the instrumentality of the parent, the parent and the subsidiary may be regarded, for tax purposes, as a single entity.[59]

The number of subsidiaries that a tax-exempt organization may have for the purpose of conducting business activities is not fixed by law. Thus, an exempt organization may house, in one or more for-profit subsidiaries, business activities that are far more extensive than the exempt functions. Whether or not any of the business activities will be attributed to the exempt organization will depend on the particular facts and circumstances—i.e., whether through interlocking directorates or otherwise, one or more of the subsidiaries are deemed mere instrumentalities of the parent exempt organization.

When considering the use of a related taxable subsidiary, several tax-planning considerations must be resolved, including the capitalization of the subsidiary, the managers of the subsidiary, and the flow of income from the subsidiary to the exempt parent.

As to capitalization, the parent tax-exempt organization must be certain that an undue portion of its charitable assets is not being transferred to the subsidiary.

As to the management of the subsidiary, the IRS will attribute the activities of the subsidiary to the parent, for the purpose of assessing the ongoing tax-exempt status of the parent, if the parent is involved in the day-to-day management of the subsidiary, thereby making the subsidiary an instrumentality of the parent. (Such an attribution, of course, defeats the purpose for establishing the subsidiary.) A majority interlock of directors between parent and subsidiary may alone cause the IRS to find the presence of day-to-day management by the tax-exempt parent, thereby imputing the subsidiary's activities to the parent, which in turn may lead to loss of the parent's tax-exempt status.

If the taxable subsidiary is a for-profit corporation, the parent owns it by holding all or a controlling portion of its stock. If the taxable subsidiary is a nonexempt, nonprofit

57. Moline Properties, Inc. v. Commissioner, 319 U.S. 436 (1943).
58. Britt v. United States, 431 F.2d 227 (5th Cir. 1970).
59. Krivo Industrial Supply Co. v. National Distillers and Chemical Corp., 483 F.2d 1098 (5th Cir. 1973).

organization, the parent owns it by means of overlapping directorates (with the above-discussed danger of attribution of activities), by holding all or a controlling portion of its stock (assuming it is formed in a state that authorizes stock-based nonprofits), or by being the sole member.

As to the transfer of funds from a taxable subsidiary to an exempt parent, that income will be taxable as unrelated income to the parent if it is interest, rents, royalties, annuities, or capital gain, where the parent has (directly or indirectly) 80 percent or more control of the subsidiary.[60] However, if the subsidiary pays dividends to the parent, the dividends are not taxable to the parent because they are not deductible by the subsidiary.

Use of a separately incorporated subsidiary also offers the further opportunity for sheltering from some forms of personal liability those individuals who serve as the directors and officers of the subsidiary. Moreover, there may be, with the for-profit subsidiary, the ability to maintain compensation arrangements for the key employees that would not be appropriate for nonprofit organizations.

CONCLUSION

As tax-exempt organizations endeavor to generate additional revenue in these days of declining governmental support, proposed adverse tax reform, more sophisticated management, and greater pressure for more services, they are increasingly drawn to fee-for-service activities, some of which may be unrelated to their exempt activities.

This phenomenon, coupled with the increasing proclivity of the courts to find activities unrelated because they are "commercial" and the growing unrest over "competition" between tax-exempt organizations and for-profit entities, is clear evidence that this aspect of exempt organizations law is quickly evolving and is on the way to being reshaped, partly by the U.S. Congress.

Indeed, congressional hearings that have explored the entrepreneurial activities of tax-exempt organizations and the contemporary application of the unrelated income rules have taken place before the Oversight Subcommittee of the House Ways and Means Committee. Other such hearings are imminent. One of the purposes of these hearings is to examine the allegations that tax-exempt organizations are unfairly competing with for-profit organizations.

These inquiries will force revisitation of the rationale for the tax exemption of certain types of nonprofit organizations, and a look at whether some existing tax exemptions are outmoded, and whether some new forms of tax-exempt status are required.

However, the principal focus of the hearing, in addition to the competition issue, will be the ongoing efficacy of the unrelated income rules, and the establishment and use by tax-exempt organizations of subsidiaries, partnerships, and other ventures.

Also to be explored are whether the IRS has an adequate and balanced enforcement program in this area, the portion of unrelated income that is actually reported to the

60. IRC §512(b)(13).

government, and whether the existing tax forms (annual information return Form 990 and unrelated income tax return Form 990-T) are adequate to identify the relatedness of business activities and satisfy other compliance needs.

Interest in this federal tax law topic is growing fast, and all indications are that this trend will continue. Indeed, the matter of nonprofit enterprise is the most important aspect of existing and changing tax law principles facing the nonprofit community today.

2

How to Think About Enterprise

EDWARD SKLOOT

WHAT ARE THE KEY ISSUES involved in developing an entrepreneurial venture? What risks must be taken? For what long-term reward? Each nonprofit organization must confront these questions and answer them for itself, in order to determine whether the products and services it wants to bring to the marketplace are commercially viable.

Relatively few nonprofit organizations approach entrepreneurship convinced that they can succeed. A more common feeling is caution, often laced with anxiety, as to whether and how to proceed. Every opportunity presents both enticements and hazards. One thing is sure, however; ventures should *never* be started for the wrong reasons.

THE "WRONG REASONS"

The first wrong reason is financial weakness or desperation. A substantial number of nonprofit organizations come to entrepreneurship out of desperation. With tight or declining budgets, now or anticipated, they suspect that selling products or services might provide a quick form of financial salvation.

This approach would scarcely be worthy of mention were it not so familiar. Yet the fact is, earned income ventures need organizational stability and financial strength in order to be developed, nurtured, established, and run. The fragile nonprofit bent on enterprise will only damage itself and create greater instability in seeking entrepreneurial solutions to systemic funding problems.

Enterprise development must derive from healthy balance sheets, income, and cash flow statements in order to be viable. Start-up dollars must be in-hand and the commitment to provide necessary resources must be present. Moreover, since ventures

27

are likely to take many months (or even years) to reach profitability, earned income strategies seldom can provide a quick fix for the at-risk organization.

The second wrong reason is the existence of apparent demand for an organization's products or services. Typical cases are when handbooks, manuals, or videotapes seem to be "selling like hotcakes," or when requests for referrals, consultations, or placements appear to be increasing at a rapid rate. Staff members become convinced that they can sell the product or service at a real profit.

The problem is that these indicators of demand are superficial and, by themselves, are highly suspect. They tell little about such matters as fixed costs, price sensitivity, actual or potential competition, and long-term market demand. No product or service is as profitable or easy to market as at first perceived, and nonprofits should resist the urge to "go commercial" without thorough internal, environmental, and market analyses.

The third wrong reason is the assumption that ventures will always bring favorable publicity, which will then attract new funders or supporters. Implicit in this thought is the idea that even if ventures lose money, they may well have another use—helping to improve fund-raising.

This thinking is flawed as well, and for at least three reasons. First, ventures don't always bring favorable publicity. They may fail; upset a community group, a local businessman, or other constituency; or just not make much of an impact. Second, favorable publicity does not necessarily translate into increased support. Third, and most important, the concept that it is permissible to lose money makes little sense under any circumstances. Nonprofit organizations can no more afford to fail in their entrepreneurial activity than for-profits can. If the organization goes into a venture anticipating a loss, it no doubt will suffer one.

A final wrong reason is pressure to enter venturing from members of the board or special constituencies. Pet projects may be distracting to the organization and financially foolhardy. One case in point was an arts organization that was pressed to accept a donation of extremely attractive, original posters for sale to members and ticket purchasers. The organization resisted, knowing that the availability of product was only the first step toward successful venturing. Even the simplest, easiest sale takes longer to accomplish and needs more staff time and money than at first presumed. Operating officers and boards of directors should thus scrutinize every gift horse for actual and potential value as well as for hidden development costs.

THINKING ABOUT VENTURING

The only "right reason" to move into enterprise is this: *the anticipated financial reward is worth the risk*. All other concerns, including the current and projected financial strength of the organization, the "ethical" appropriateness of the venture, and the availability of managerial talent, can be studied under this risk-and-reward framework. By evaluating risk and reward, an organization can judge whether staff are capable and supportive, whether financing is available, and whether the likelihood of success is worth the effort.

Some venturing ideas, of course, are preposterous, while others skirt the line of legality or appropriateness. They can be dropped without a second thought.

Assessing risk is an analytic task, not a metaphysical judgment. Occasionally one encounters nonprofit executives, board members, or their constituents who almost viscerally react to the prospect of enterprise. Some argue that it will "taint" the organization or drive it away from its exempt mission. This is a valid concern. Where the compromises are too great, the organization should not proceed, and, in many instances, the taint is simply too obvious to ignore. Yet the answers to these ethical concerns are not always clear. Most earned income activity does not *ipso facto* compromise an organization's exempt mission, and most will not taint it.

At one time or another, the gift shop of the Metropolitan Museum of Art, the mint and cookie sales of the Girl Scouts of America, the licensed products of the Children's Television Workshop's "Sesame Street," and the corporate employee assistance programs of several national service organizations were criticized as compromising their exempt mission. In hindsight, most of the criticism seems to have been a debate over personal taste and views of quality. Meanwhile, the financial strength of these organizations has been measurably improved.

Risk is the exposure to loss. It can be measured, usually in terms of dollars. The higher the risk, the greater the likelihood of financial (and organizational) failure. Ultimately, for earned income ventures, questions of risk are handled in a business plan. (See the chapters by Cynthia W. Massarsky and Ellen Arrick for development of the business plan and financing issues.) A business plan seeks to minimize the exposure to loss and maximize the possibility of financial gain. Every step in the process of developing a business plan, as well as in developing the business itself, has its own degree of risk.

For example, the executives of a large outpatient clinic for the mentally disabled perceived an opportunity in starting a sheltered workshop on the site of their day-treatment center. They sought to minimize the risk to the organization by hiring a consultant to assess 1) the kinds of work and workload the clients could handle; 2) the extra supervisory and administrative costs that would be required at a given level of work; and 3) the existence of other, local competitors. The research found that the workload its clients could handle was light, that the new internal costs would be substantial, that the client base would need high levels of supervision in order to work in a sheltered workshop setting, and that there might be opportunities to informally subcontract with another area workshop to test the opportunity under limited, controlled conditions.

Thus, the clinic paid a modest amount for useful research (low risk) and saved itself from moving too quickly into a larger and far more risky endeavor. It also uncovered a viable alternative that could test the opportunity in graduated increments.

The risk to the organization can also be measured by comparison with other venturing or even fund-raising possibilities. For example, a nonprofit organization might have $100,000 (or $10,000 or $1 million) available to earn more money. It has several options. One possibility is to deposit the funds in a local savings bank and earn interest. Another is to purchase an insured certificate of deposit. Passively earning steady income at a fixed annual percentage, with virtually no chance of loss, may offer a less risky and more desirable alternative to investing in an earned income venture. Another option is to use part or all of the funds for a fund-raising benefit that might net several hundred thousand dollars. The point is that every organization has several income-earning alternatives encompassing several levels of risk, and that enterprise is only one of these options. Further, each option can be weighed against the others in terms of potential for payback.

Risk also has a time dimension. The longer it takes to reach specific financial goals, the greater the likelihood of increased problems and failure. Furthermore, the longer it takes to achieve financial success (all things being equal), the less the value of the money when it finally is in hand. For example, a fund-raising event or a direct mail solicitation might consume six months, but the return will be immediate and clear. On the other hand, creating a successful venture might take several years—and the financial results might be no greater than those of the fund-raising event, which might be presented several more times before the venture pans out. The *time value* of money, then, is an important calculation (not to speak of inflation), for it may be better to earn a smaller amount sooner than a larger amount later.

The concept of *proportionality* is also a valuable one in these early assessments. The size of a venture should correspond in some proportionate way to the size of the organization. In general, smaller organizations should seek smaller-size ventures and take very modest risks to achieve financial reward. Small nonprofits have fewer cash reserves and human resources, and are likely to be financially more vulnerable than multimillion dollar organizations. Larger organizations may have greater flexibility to choose the size of their venture, although for them the smaller the enterprise, the lower the relative return—and the less attractive the payback. For large organizations, small ventures may not be worth doing.

Early in the venture conceptualization process, key executives and board members should agree upon a dollar amount the organization should earn over time. The decision might be, "We'd like to earn $25,000 annually after a fifteen-month start-up phase, and double that amount by the third year of operation." Another response might be, "We want to be in the black immediately, and to make 10 percent of our operating budget by the second year." This agreement on the financial target of an enterprise can help do two things: first, it can establish a collective vision that will enhance communication and diminish misunderstanding over expectations, and, second, it can let the executives dispose of inappropriate or impractical proposals as being outside the targeted reward.

FOUR BASIC QUESTIONS

There are four questions to ask. The answers will determine whether the rewards will be worth the risks.[1]

---

[1] I am indebted to Professor Zenas Block of the New York University Graduate School of Business Administration for this formulation of the questions. The answers are mine. See his "Can Corporate Venturing Succeed?" in the *Journal of Business Strategy*, vol. 3, no. 2, Fall, 1982, pp. 21–33.

What are the risks involved and can we afford to take them?

This first question is a logical extension of the foregoing discussion of risk. The risks come in several forms, including financial, organizational, and reputational; there is also risk to the overall morale of the organization.

The financial risks have several aspects. The first is that the venture may cost more to plan, start, and operate than the organization is willing or able to commit. While several earned income activities may have developed almost as an afterthought (such as a book, videotape, or new use for an old product), these activities are usually the exception to the rule. They commonly have value because the marketplace demands them in precisely the form in which they were developed.

All long-term, market-driven enterprises have some development and planning costs. As noted, these costs must be assessed at the earliest possible point, and from two vantage points. The first is the dollar cost of the contemplated venture. This is the more narrow viewpoint and it is spelled out in a business plan. The second is the opportunity cost, i.e., where the money might otherwise be spent.

Financial risk may involve seeking additional resources through loans or through the sale of equity to investors. Long-term relationships with bankers or even shareholders means less control for the nonprofit over its assets since they have the right by previous agreement to call in or sell their investment at a particular time. If the venture loses money, it may damage the ability of the organization to fulfill its exempt purposes.

A second area of risk is organizational. The new venture may demand constant attention from numerous staff members, particularly in its start-up phase. The development director, the public relations professional, and the senior program staff may be called on to pitch in. It may well be hard to know where the enterprise fits, or to position it easily, and the greater the attention the venture receives, the greater the stress may be on the organization itself. The risk is that the venture competes for time and money with activities closer to the exempt mission of the organization.

A third area of risk is in the area of reputation. For many nonprofit leaders, this is one of the most important (and least measurable) concerns. The nonprofit organization has a "persona," which speaks to its board, its clients, its local community, and its funders. Entrepreneurial ventures often raise fears that the reputation of the organization will be damaged, that it will be seen as a grasping, acquisitive sell-out, and that this characterization will apply *whether or not* the organization earns money.

In part, good planning can deal with some of this risk. Surveys can do much to clarify what the relevant constituencies think about the organization and whether venturing will be greeted favorably. Presentations to key constituents can improve understanding and gain support. No nonprofit can blithely move into earned income activity in a consequential way without being sure that its traditional friends will remain faithful to its cause. Bankers and funders, for example, may become more resistant to supporting the organization if it appears to be financially reckless in the use of its assets.

Conversely, successful venturing can measurably enhance the reputation of the nonprofit. Successful ventures may not only earn income for the organization, but they may also enhance its image as a talented, creative, and market-oriented winner. Bankers and funders, communities and constituents, all like winners.

A final risk involves morale. For some nonprofits, the exempt mission is all. The purity of the cause binds staff and board and focuses their attention on service delivery. An entrepreneurial venture may stoke resistance by staff and board who may, whether the venture is successful or not, feel sold out. Indeed, in some organizations, the greater the financial success, the greater the potential for this feeling.

What are the resources, skills, and knowledge required and can we supply them?

The resources, skills, and knowledge are often expensive to acquire. They need not be a permanent part of the organization; consultants, volunteers, or board members may supply them, for a fee or *pro bono*.

Say a hospital wants to establish a gift shop. Its executives, board members, doctors, nurses, and other staff have spent their careers providing health care, not in running a retail venture. The first thing required is knowledge of the retail industry, with a particular focus on gift shops. The organization may conclude that the knowledge does not exist in-house and must be acquired. Other kinds of knowledge are also needed in design and planning, law, marketing, financial management, etc. The organization must assess the knowledge it possesses in-house and decide how to add the missing information.

One reason why so many businesses start small is that it may be costly to acquire skills and knowledge in all of these areas at once. Organizations should consciously choose to calibrate their level of effort and the size of the enterprise to the talent they have available. This is why proportionality is so important. Disproportionate amounts of consulting assistance suggest that the venture may be too large for the organization to manage well. They also imply that at some point the resources, skills, and knowledge must be institutionalized at substantial cost.

An organization must assess its needs in venturing. It should evaluate whether the resources, skills, and knowledge are available, and, if not, the cost of acquiring them. Many of these needs are identified in the planning process, through a feasibility study, and, ultimately, through a business plan.

How do our values, goals and attitudes differ from those required to support the venture, and can we adapt?

For some nonprofit organizations, this is *the* key question.

The value system in nonprofit organizations commonly rests on an important concept of service and public participation. As a result, staff and board members may be more interested in fulfilling their exempt mission and providing service than in earning money for the organization. Their attitudes toward enterprise may reflect those values. For some, earning money has a distinctly untoward or offensive character. For others, work satisfaction compensates for higher salaries derived from earned income. For all these persons, enterprise may not be an easy flag around which they can rally.

In the last five years, as financial worries of nonprofits have increased, and as entrepreneurship has become more acceptable, the distance between the *venturers* and the *service deliverers* has narrowed. As greater numbers of organizations start their own earned income activities (or joint venture them with for-profit corporations), the resistance to the idea of entrepreneurship diminishes. This is not to argue that venturing is appropriate most of the time for most nonprofit organizations, but that familiarity and understanding, informed by financial pressures and opportunity, have greatly diminished the resistance to earning money.

Resistance deriving from value conflicts must be dealt with seriously. If the value system (and corporate culture) is totally unyielding, venturing should not be pressed. Doing so can produce serious internal conflicts, morale problems, and perhaps even diminished service capability. On the other hand, if a willingness exists to discuss the issue of venturing, there are several useful approaches.

First, the idea can be introduced in forums that are receptive. Proponents of venturing, like all new or controversial ideas, must choose their audiences and build support for their projects. Small groups of interested board members or staff might be a more appropriate setting for research and discussion of venturing until the specific business plan is ready to be unveiled.

Second, examples of enterprises in the service field of the organization can be provided; for example, in the arts or health and human services. They indicate the viability of venturing among comparable organizations. Visits and on-site discussions can be arranged.

Third, expectations of financial gain can be kept at a modest level. Entrepreneurship trumpeted as financial salvation for the organization only asks for trouble. Finally, the positive financial contributions that enterprise can make to an organization's programs should be discussed, to underscore the link between financial reward and program enhancement.

To be sure, the employees of an organization may give lip service to a venture while choosing not to support it. This passive sabotage will gradually erode a venture and is a risk to be assessed in the planning process. For the fact is that in some nonprofits the attitudes toward risk (the lower the better) and enterprise (the less the better) may be so strong as to predispose it away from enterprise and toward alternative approaches to income generation.

What are the timing requirements for launching the venture and can they be met?

The success of a venture opportunity may hinge on the speed by which it can be introduced and expanded. This timing question has two facets: the demand of the external marketplace and internal capacity of the organization to satisfy it.

The external marketplace may be ripe for a new product or service. The number of potential entrants may be large. For example, growth in the home health care market, and its case management submarket, has opened up real opportunity for human service organizations and private vendors. At the same time, the marketplace in any particular locale or neighborhood may be limited in size and rapidly saturated. This puts pressure on an organization to act quickly, to garner a substantial market share, and to expand upon its position before competitors enter the field.

The nonprofit should assess the competitive environment, actual and projected, and the expected duration of the entry opportunity. It also should determine, in its business plan, the market share it wants and the expense that will be involved in garnering it. It should then assess its internal capacity to enter the marketplace.

A case in point was a national service organization that produced and marketed a set of science kits for the elementary school market. It learned that another nonprofit, a large museum, was readying itself to enter the market. There was nothing proprietary about the material in the kits or the teaching curriculum of either organization. A serious competitive advantage could have been achieved by entering the marketplace first and cementing purchasing arrangements with local school boards and science curriculum specialists. For this organization, the timing issue was important. Had product development time been gradual and the costs spread over several years, the organization could easily have acquired a dominant market position. However, the entry of the other organization forced it to contemplate the current availability of staff, as well as of cash, and it decided to pursue a smaller, local market at much less risk.

The pressure of time may be positive or negative. It can force an organization to "get serious" about its venturing schemes and create policies and programs that expand earned income. On the other hand, pressure can push an organization toward hasty decision making and poor planning, which lay the groundwork for later failure.

THE CHAMPION AND THE PLANNING TEAM

Every venture, like every new service or program, must have a champion to succeed. Given numerous competing projects, insufficient time to accomplish all the organization's goals, and the normal level of inertia found in all organizations, only a convinced, well-placed individual (or individuals) can produce a venturing success. Although success cannot be guaranteed, the individual's relentless advocacy and skill are the *sine qua non* of a positive outcome.

The champion need not be the chief executive officer (CEO) of the organization. However, the person should be visible and close to the locus of influence. The person's position might be that of chief operating officer, vice-president, senior program director, or even board member.

At some point, generally as a venture opportunity begins to require development funds and a time commitment from more than one key person, the champion, if he or she is not the CEO, must win the leader's support. Furthermore, the closer the venture gets to actual start-up, the greater the need to increase the circle of participants through a planning team. This team will share the analytic tasks and create internal support for the enterprise.

The planning team need not be large. Two or three persons may be sufficient, depending on time available and planning needs. The team should be appointed and work under the authority of the CEO, or possibly that of a special planning group of board members. The team should have specific tasks to accomplish in specific time frames. Experience has shown that lackadaisical planning efforts are rarely successful, and that once a decision is made to proceed with a venture, it must be tracked and moved with dispatch.

In a sense, the planning team must become the "owners" of the venture concept. Although they may have no personal financial stake in the project, they must be personally committed to producing results in a timely manner. Ultimately, the planning team may become the collective champion of the venture.

The team may choose to hire consultants to address various aspects of the venturing concept. Consultants can inject knowledge, skills, and resources into the planning process. It is important to use them sparingly, however.

The planning team should never give up ownership of the idea to a consultant. Specialized, outside help is best used when tasks are finite and clear and when they are well supervised by the planning team. The greater the delegation of analytic tasks to outsiders, the lower the venture's chance of success, since full-time staff members must ultimately be responsible for starting and operating the venture itself. They need to be actively involved from the beginning.

Financing the planning activities may be costly. Substantial ventures imply a considerable dollar outlay—itself a risk to the organization. In general, these early costs will have to be paid for with internally generated funds. The earliest stages of venture planning are the most difficult to finance. Banks are unlikely to lend for this purpose, even if current relationships are strong. Venture capitalists enter the process much later, if at all, as do likely vendors and potential customers. Still, there are several places to look for planning money.

The first place to investigate is the operating budget of the organization. Rarely is there no spare cash for an important project. If no planning dollars can be made available, this is an indication of the importance of the venture to the nonprofit. The organization that is strapped for cash at this stage must wonder whether it will ever have the resources to commit to an enterprise.

The nonprofit should prepare a budget for the planning phase. It may choose to dip into its fund balance, or keep a position or two unfilled temporarily and use the funds that are saved. It might take an unanticipated gift or bequest and earmark it for venture planning. There are numerous paths to internal finance, as the creative executive knows.

Two other sources, less common, are also plausible. The first are members of the board who may choose to contribute money, individually or collectively, to the investigation of an enterprise. Board members may set up a pool of money or even make a challenge grant to be used for this purpose. The second source is the foundation community, which may be receptive to a proposal to fund the planning process. Although foundations are generally reluctant to make grants for this purpose, a few, particularly those that are long-time supporters of the organization, may be receptive to the request.

As the venturing idea works its way toward actual operation, increasing amounts of time of the chief executive officer will be absorbed in planning the enterprise. If the venture involves little risk, if it is small relative to the budget or the resources made available, the involvement of the executive may be modest. But for a venture that involves substantial risk (in dollars, value changes, and scarce resources, etc.) the CEO may expect to spend between 20 percent and 50 percent of his or her time for several months attending to problems inherent in the planning phase.

Thus, a key question for the organization is whether the CEO (and/or key staff) can be detailed to devote substantial amounts of time to the early stages of venture development. The CEO who is over his head with financial and program issues cannot be expected to champion a risky entrepreneurial venture. Furthermore, as a practical matter, the CEO cannot be expected to spend time and use all his "chits" with colleagues and board members (who are themselves absorbed in other concerns) to get them to attend to enterprise.

3

The Venture Planning Process

EDWARD SKLOOT

IT IS WIDELY BELIEVED by executives of nonprofit organizations that raw energy and lofty motives can make a success of almost any endeavor. At least with regard to nonprofit enterprise, this is a false and even dangerous assumption, for several reasons.

First, enterprise demands knowledge of a set of business skills that must be implemented in a systematic, disciplined fashion. For nonprofits unused to dealing in a market economy, where success is governed by bottom-line considerations, the pitfalls are numerous. For example, nonprofits may have to deal with brokers, bankers, or factors; manage cash flow on a regular basis; borrow prudently; and repay promptly. If they are in a retail venture, they may have to price competitively, take markdowns, slash inventory, and offer premiums. Business *is* different from nonprofit service delivery, and mastery of how it runs is the irreducible core of success.

Second, the reputation of the organization for good works is seldom sufficient to sustain a business venture. At best, customers will buy a product or service once on the strength of the standing of the organization's reputation. If the quality of what they buy is inferior, all the goodwill in the world will not induce them to purchase again. There would be no Girl Scout cookies, and a much diminished Girl Scout organization, if the product were not consistently superior.

Third, the world of business is ever changing. Day-to-day operating problems constantly threaten to upset even the best-laid plans. Orders don't arrive; bills do. Poor weather drastically cuts traffic and sales. Key employees get sick or move on to better jobs and must be replaced immediately. Creditors press for payment. The headaches and pleasures of commercial venturing, large and small, are constant and often unforgiving. Accordingly, nonprofits have to be ready to learn their business and work at it constantly in order to successfully play in the marketplace.

THE EIGHT STAGES OF BUSINESS

All ventures, regardless of their form of ownership, must progress through at least eight stages in order to be successful. These stages apply to ventures of *any* size. The small museum shop must pass through them no less than the personal computer business of IBM.

Stage 1: Defining the Business. No venture can succeed without a clear articulation of the business. This is commonly done through a written business plan. The business plan is a comprehensive description of the proposed exchange of services or products. It is discussed at length in the chapters by Cynthia W. Massarsky and Ellen Arrick.

Stage 2: Creating the Organization. The organization should reflect the conception of its founders and it should accurately mirror their purposes. It should link the board and staff of the nonprofit organization in a way that serves them as well as the venture. For example, the establishment of overlapping board memberships may be mutually enhancing. The organization should be commensurate in size with the venture—neither so big as to overwhelm it in hierarchy nor so small as to be ineffective in decision making.

Stage 3: Raising Capital. The venture—start-up or ongoing—needs money to run it. Capital has two important facets. First is the absolute *amount* of dollars, say $250,000 in a working capital loan. Second is the *timing* of the money, i.e., when it is available for use. For example, if the business must pay cash to its vendors (a frequent occurrence for start-ups with no commercial track record), a loan that comes in slowly, or six months after the venture has begun, may simply be too late to help the business. One of the most important causes of small business failures is cash flow problems that arise from the late receipt of money or the poor management of receivables.

Stage 4: Creating and Maintaining the Market Niche. This is the market analysis and marketing strategy component of the venture. By segmenting, targeting, attracting and retaining customers (Professor Philip Kotler of Northwestern University calls this the "STAR System"), the venture's position in the marketplace can be identified, maintained, and enhanced. Obviously, the more successful the venture, the more competitors (actual or potential) will find the business an attractive opportunity. A profitable business can be complacent only at the risk of losing its market niche to the competition.

Stage 5: Hiring and Retaining the Management Team. Management is the crucial ingredient. Especially in nonprofit organizations, where business skills are commonly in short supply, the caliber of management will make or break the enterprise. Every effort should be made to identify the best persons for the job, and to compensate them at rates of pay that will keep them committed to the venture. If the venture is established in-house, the issue of staff compensation will have especially serious implications for morale and productivity throughout the organization.

Stage 6: Marketing the Enterprise. Every conceivable cost-effective vehicle for putting the venture before the targeted audience should be utilized. For some nonprofits the approach might be through direct mail; for others it might well be personal selling. The value of free publicity cannot be underestimated and should always be sought.

Stage 7: Expanding the Business. When the venture has become a serious presence in the marketplace and has been integrated into the organization, it must ultimately move to secure its position by expanding its product or service line, or its clientele. In general, no business can survive by standing still. Expansion produces staffing opportunities and makes the organization stronger by diversifying its offerings. The venture must be careful not to grow too quickly, however, stretching its human and financial resources beyond their capacity.

Stage 8: Course Correcting. This stage is really part and parcel of all the others. All aspects of the enterprise should constantly be reviewed, and action taken when projections are not met. Re-calibration is the rule, not the exception, since no business, from day one, works as planned. In this sense, then, the most important ingredient of success is *adaptability to the marketplace,* for if the enterprise cannot move quickly to meet a constantly changing environment, it will not remain profitable for long.

FINDING THE BUSINESS THAT IS RIGHT

From the nonprofits' standpoint, there are only four options for business development. As depicted in Table I, nonprofits can improve on what they are currently doing, create a new product or service for an old market, find a new market for an old product or service, or create a new product or service for an entirely new market.

An example of an improvement of an ongoing service (no. 1) is upgrading a home health care service with newly trained staff, and charging an increased fee for it (or, perhaps, starting to charge for a formerly free service). An example of creating a new product or service for old markets (no. 2) is introducing tours and day trips for an organization's membership or alumni association. Finding new markets for an old product or service (no. 3) may include expanding the audience for regional theatre or ballet by attracting corporate members, "yuppies," or senior citizens. Finally, creating

TABLE I. FOUR OPTIONS FOR BUSINESS DEVELOPMENT

	Old Product or Service	New Product or Service
Old Customer Base	1	2
New Customer Base	3	4

a new product or service for new markets (no. 4) might involve developing a piece of computer software for young children by a traditional educational institution.

The degree of difficulty rises with the numbers. The first option is the easiest to accomplish. It is closest to what the nonprofit already does well. The more familiar and institutionalized a product or service is to an organization, the less trouble it will have creating a business with it. Institutional familiarity is an asset to be respected, and nonprofit organizations should focus here first for guidance and inspiration.

There is often an unstated bias toward creating a new product or service. People often assume that newness is attractive and that attractiveness is easy to sell. It is seldom so simple, however. In many cases, especially where the customers are not used to purchasing, a new product or service is very hard to market.

The fourth option is the most risky one—to create a new product or service for an entirely new market. This is vastly different from trying to find a new source of customers for old products or services, or developing a new product or service for old customers.

The nonprofit dance company that has discovered a way to construct modular housing for low-income citizens, and tries to do it, is asking for trouble. The organization for the physically or emotionally disabled that tries to run its own retail outlet with its own clients is on shaky ground. A useful principle, then, for for-profit corporations as much as for nonprofit organizations, is to do what one does best. The greater the departure from established ways, the greater the problems in achieving commercial success.

The most important consideration for the nonprofit organization contemplating enterprise is to minimize risk. Contrary to much conventional wisdom, risk can be measured rather precisely, and one function of preparing a business plan is to identify and squeeze out all unnecessary risk. Equally, the potential reward can also be measured. Every nonprofit organization should balance off the risk and reward of the contemplated enterprise, and then place the calculation in the context of its exempt mission, before it proceeds full-speed ahead. The sequence of steps by which organizational commitment is gradually increased is discussed below.

THE INTERNAL AUDIT

Early in the venturing process, the organization should undertake an internal audit. This audit reveals the working environment of the nonprofit, which should be analyzed to uncover all impediments to venturing. The investigation should be performed systematically, assisted by means of a written checklist, and the results evaluated dispassionately. If the organization cannot see its way clear to remedying the internal problems identified, an earned-income venture will only exacerbate its problems. Table II contains a suggested audit checklist, which can be modified to fit the specific character of the nonprofit organization.

Obviously, the answers to the checklist are complex, and some may be easier to derive than others. What *exactly* does trustee support mean? How flexible *is* the

TABLE II. CHECKLIST FOR AN INTERNAL AUDIT TO BE PERFORMED
BEFORE ESTABLISHING AN ENTERPRISE

	Weak				Strong
	1	2	3	4	5

Personnel
    Staff interest in concept
    Staff experience in business
    Staff "mentality"
    Trustee support
    Member support
    Alignment on exempt goals
    Availability of executive director
    Availability of financial staff

Total A _____

Finances
    Fiscal stability—past 3 years of budgets
    Diversity of revenue sources
    Flexibility in budget/ability to free-up seed funds
    Ability to free-up working capital
    Likelihood of future support from current supporters

Total B _____

Facilities
    Availability of space in current facility (now and future)
    Location in building
    Location in neighborhood
    Attractiveness
    Room for expansion
    State of repair
    Overhead/equipment availability

Total C _____

Systems
    MIS in operation
    Data collection expertise

Total D _____

Special Assets (Examples)
    Reputation
    Trademark, copyright, etc.
    Fidelity of customers
    Usable contacts
    National network/chapters
    Credit/borrowing power
    Other (list and rank)

Total E _____

budget? What contacts will *really* be helpful? Although there is some unclarity in every response, it is imperative that the organization be as precise as possible in its responses. It may be useful to answer every sub-area of every section with a one-page statement, enumerating the specifics of each strength and weakness. Upon completion, each statement can be used to focus on corrective actions.

Some organizations will score well in one or two areas and show pronounced weakness in others. The tendency in most organizations is to ignore the weak spots and expect, or hope, that the venture's momentum will carry the organization along to success. This is an erroneous belief. Efforts must be made to deal with internal problems before they negatively affect operations.

Some audits will take weeks to complete. Obviously, too, the exercise has uses beyond establishing the internal viability of a venturing idea. For one thing, it can provide a reasonably accurate profile of the organization's overall health and suggest areas that need strengthening. The paramount point as it affects entrepreneurial activity, however, is that if any part of the investigation comes up irretrievably negative, the organization can drop the venture idea before a costly commitment is made.

PROJECT IDENTIFICATION AND IDEA REFINEMENT

While the internal audit is underway, the organization will probably be in the process of identifying or refining its entrepreneurial idea. Although most nonprofits will not be wholly devoid of venturing ideas, all may find it useful to "scan and screen" the horizon to identify all the related ideas they can. Even with the one "hot" venture and the enthusiasm ready to make it work, the organization should remain committed to a systematic process of investigation of venture options.

It is useful to think of the venture creation process as a big funnel. Everyone and everything starts at the top, at a level of much raw data and plenty of ideas. The venture development process is little more than working many good ideas down through the funnel until the very best one drops out, is selected, and a strategy for its implementation is designed. It is the *channeling process* that is vital to evaluating the risks involved in proceeding. At each step, the organization can decide to continue the endeavor, choose another enterprise, or drop out altogether.

CASE I

Educational Research Institute

The Educational Research Institute (ERI), a nonprofit educational organization, provides new and updated information for farmers interested in converting from the heavy, systematic use of chemical fertilizer to organic fertilizer or no fertilizer at all. Currently, ERI publishes a successful journal and engages in research, under contract, for private- and public-sector clients. The organization exists on journal revenue and contributions from foundations and corporations. What other related projects might be contemplated in order to diversify the income base of the organization?

One area of possible venturing is for the organization to do more publishing, i.e., to develop publishing-related products for its current base of customers, which include farmers, governments, and corporations (Table I, no. 2). The organization could do many things. Here are a few of them:

- Write *manuals* and *handbooks* for farmers on conversion to organic farming
- Distribute and *sell* government publications (nationally and internationally)
- Create a *book club* for subscribers to its journal, or for others, in the area of organic farming
- Write a *newsletter* on trends in organic farming for agribusiness
- Prepare an *in-house newsletter* for one or several commercial clients
- Establish a *features-news service* to service regional and local newspapers
- Write or consult on writing *textbooks* on farming-related subjects for high schools and colleges
- Prepare and market a fertilizer-use *data base* for governments.

Since the information ERI possesses serves its educational purpose, it might well consider doing other related, educational ventures as well. It could do the following:

- Produce *audio tapes* for farmers to listen to while farming
- Design and create *computer software* on optimizing the use of fertilizer and nonfertilizer inputs
- Offer *courses and workshops* for farmers, agriculture students, journalists, etc., on organic farming
- Conduct *field trips* and run *field days* to visit operating, successful organic farms
- Establish a readers' *information service* on articles and books in the field, perhaps for a membership fee
- Set up a telephone *hot line* for problem solving
- Produce a *radio show*
- Run national and international *conferences* for various market segments, etc.

The ERI example demonstrates, by analogy, that there are numerous possibilities for organizations seeking to identify entrepreneurial activities related to their mission and current activities. As a result of this scanning (or brainstorming) process, organizations should be able to identify and then weed out viable venture possibilities. Since at the top of the funnel the data are plentiful but unsystematically arrayed, nonprofit executives should be particularly attuned to using their intuitive sense of what might produce success, as well as their analytic ability.

The next step in the scanning and screening process is simple—and extremely important. It should be done by organizations that already have their one idea identified too. A senior staff person should write down the business concept, in no more than two pages and preferably less, detailing exactly how the business will work. The process of translating a concept to paper, and then spelling it out fully, does several useful things.

First, it stimulates detailed thought about the viability of the idea. Flaws and problems appear reasonably quickly in a poor but seductive idea. Second, the writing process stimulates communication among staff members who may be charged with developing the business concept. Third, writing it down helps begin the process of identifying the resources the organization may need for entry into the marketplace. Fourth, writing it down implicitly raises the question, "Is this what we really want to do?" If one large fund-raising dinner could net twice the dollars with one-third the effort, then the organization might seriously consider dropping the venture concept. Finally, writing the idea down forces advocates and opponents with the organization to go beyond the level of "cocktail talk" and toward the point of reasoned analysis. Thus, by assigning responsibility for producing an imagined version of the up-and-running business, the organization takes a large step forward in its risk-and-reward analysis.

THE FIRST-CUT CALCULATION

As suggested in an earlier chapter, key officials of the organization should try to agree on an income target. As a practical matter, the answer to the question "How much do you want to make?" cannot be "As much as possible."

Nonprofit executives should quickly remove some of the mystery and romance from their contemplated venture and establish an income target. By doing so, they can measure the anticipated net income of the venture against their expectations and assess whether the enterprise is worth pursuing. This measuring process goes on throughout the planning effort, although it is perhaps most important the first time around. The following is a much-simplified example of a nonprofit's first-cut calculation:

CASE II

Detox, Inc.

Detox, Inc., a nonprofit social service organization, decides it wants to net $100,000 from an earned income venture. It has an annual budget of $2.5 million. It proposes to sell individual alcohol- and drug-counseling services to private corporations. The organization knows it cannot charge more than an average of $40 per session for individual counseling services.

Two large local employers, the WXYZ Corporation and the 1234 Corporation, respond to the inquiry by Detox, Inc. They expect 6 percent (or 600 employees) of their combined workforce of 10,000 employees to need the service each year; the service is comprised of ten individual sessions with a therapist/counselor. Additional support activities would be provided under another agreement. Thus, Detox, Inc., has a potential for a contract of $240,000 (600 employees × 10 sessions × $40 per session). This is its projected revenue.

The projected expenses also can be calculated. Detox, Inc., assumes that each full-time counselor can work with five clients daily (the rest of the day being spent on administrative tasks), and that each counselor would work an average of 225 days annually. Each counselor can thus handle 1,125 sessions annually, and the organization would need approximately 5.5 employees to render the service. Counselors average $25,000 annually in salary and receive fringe benefits worth 20 percent of their salary. The venture would also need one full-time administrator (at $25,000 per year plus fringes) plus a secretary (at $18,000 per year plus fringes), plus miscellaneous executive time for negotiating, marketing, etc. There would be other overhead costs as well. Basic personnel expenses under the counseling contract would look as follows:

5.5 Counselors (at $25,000)	$137,500
1 Administrator	25,000
1 Secretary	18,000
Fringes (at 20 percent)	36,000
Total personal services	$216,600

At this point, the venture planners in the organization may become skeptical of the concept. There is only $23,400 remaining in the contemplated contract to cover all other costs *and* make a profit for Detox, Inc. Suppose the remaining expenses sketch out as follows:

Executive Director's time (10 percent of salary and fringes)	$7,500
Occupancy and furniture (1,500 feet at $10/sq. ft.)	15,000
Phone/duplicating/misc.	2,500
Consultant fees/legal/accountant/etc.	2,500
Equipment/computer/service	5,000
Dues/meetings/seminars/travel	3,000
Contingency	2,500
Total nonpersonal services	$38,000
Total personal services	216,600
Total expenses	$254,600
Total income	$240,000
Profit (loss)	($14,600)

This wonderful opportunity to expand service and make a profit now looks like it will cost Detox, Inc. $14,600! Is there a business venture here?

It is worth spending additional time to reexamine each assumption and recompute each category of expense to see if the concept has any possibility of becoming even marginally profitable.

The following are a few imagined savings, or alterations to basic assumptions, which may reveal a very different opportunity:

• Detox, Inc., provides the office space and furniture to the venture—saving $15,000.

- Detox, Inc., picks up some overhead costs—saving $7,500.
- Detox, Inc., contributes the time of its bookkeeper—saving $1,000.
- Detox, Inc., proposes to make one session a group session, cutting out 530 sessions, or half the salary of a counselor, plus fringes—saving $15,000.
- Detox, Inc., decides to hire only contract labor for its counseling staff, thus eliminating the payment of fringe benefits for the five remaining counselors—saving $25,000.

Now the picture looks rather different. By "scoping out" several possible cost-cutting measures (there might well be others), the agency has reduced its projected expenses by $63,500, to $191,100. The net income to the organization (assuming it is a nonprofit division of the parent) is now $48,900—a very promising start.

This "back of the envelope" calculation of revenue and expenses provides an essential dose of reality, which tests whether a venture concept can become a viable enterprise. If the product or service is already established, or if the marketplace costs can be estimated with some precision, the entire calculation may take as little as an hour or two to perform.

One final concern must be dealt with. The organization had set a goal of earning $100,000 in the first year of the venture's operation. However, net income under this scenario will be less than half that amount. The organization may decide to adjust its income-earning expectations and consider the first year of the venture as a start-up, one that grows in earnings to $100,000 (or more) in subsequent years. Venture planners should perform similar, crude calculations for years two and three as well, to arrive at a first-cut net income figure.

MARKET RESEARCH

Assuming a decision to proceed, the organization must commit itself to researching and analyzing the market for the venture. (See the chapter by Christopher H. Lovelock and Charles B. Weinberg for a more comprehensive treatment of the subject.) Depending on the scale of the enterprise, its complexity, and its familiarity within the organization, a planning team composed of one or a few persons should be chosen. If the chief executive officer does not personally investigate the options, the person(s) delegated to do it must report directly to the CEO on a regular basis. At this point, too, a small group of board members might become involved. Some members might have particular expertise to call upon during the research and planning stage.

The involvement of the board cannot be taken lightly. Some organizations have highly competent, engaged board members, whose participation should be welcomed. Others are burdened with amateurs, some of whom may also have poor judgment. A useful rule of thumb is not to involve any more trustees than are necessary, and not to depend on them for the success of the planning process. Board members who stalwartly press a venture on an unwilling or unprepared organization are especially dangerous.

On the other hand, consulting with trustees and getting their assistance can be a useful strategy in analyzing the venture's prospects, and in coalition building for the project. Ventures are likely to take months (or years) to execute and they will need all the support they can get—particularly in an organization facing competing demands for scarce resources. Furthermore, trustees can often bring contacts, expertise, and money to encourage a venture along.

If the organization decides to set up a planning team, staff members should predominate. It may choose to hire a consultant to assist with various analytic and project management tasks, but if it chooses to do so, it must be crystal clear about what services it expects to receive. As noted in an earlier chapter, organizations that leave it to the consultant to prepare and deliver the final business plan will have great difficulty operating a venture. If the organization does not involve itself in the project from the beginning, it will not be competent to "own" it later.

Market research is an essential step in the channeling process. Research is done through primary and secondary sources to uncover every piece of relevant information on the way such a business operates.

Market research is a foreign concept to many nonprofit organizations. Many feel it is costly and time consuming. Used to identifying a *need*, and then providing a service or product to fill it, many nonprofits seldom ask the most important marketing question of all: "What does the marketplace *want*?"

The marketplace will pay for only what it wants. It is not at all obvious that people will purchase the best book on placing relatives in nursing homes, the most nurturing day care, or the most interesting avant-garde plays. In fact, it is not obvious that the marketplace wants the highest quality product or service. Market research is focused on finding out what the potential consumer base wants, what it will pay for, and what price it will pay.

Secondary market research pulls together already-existing materials. For example, a nursing home (or labor union or private school) may own a parcel of land and buildings that it currently uses as a summer camp for its patients and staff. The executives of the home have reason to believe that they could create a year-round conference center on the property, which will serve corporations and other nonprofit organizations located in the area (Table I, no. 3— new customer base for a somewhat comparable service).

The nonprofit planning team's secondary research would include a review of the literature on creating and running conference centers. Further, it would investigate directories of centers for their location, size, amenities, and price. It would research industry studies to comprehend trends in the conference center business, and key factors to successful management of them. There probably exists a conference center association whose function it is to distribute volumes of information about the conference center business. There also are house organs, brokerage house reports, magazines and newsletters in the field, and perhaps even stock-offering filings that will reveal the inner workings of the conference center business.

After completing secondary research, and sometimes overlapping it, the planning team does primary research. Primary research focuses on acquiring new information, often unavailable in the literature, which fills out the really important details of the conference center business. Personal interviews, focus groups, and surveys are the most common form of primary research, although analyses of newspaper stories, computation of available data, and direct observation ("window shopping") are also involved. Certainly several visits to nearby and/or successful centers are imperative for the organization contemplating a conference facility.

Who would one go to for interviews on the conference center marketplace or its history and trends? Among the people are retired conference center executives, association directors, journalists, stock brokers, local area merchants, potential vendors, corporate users, and even center directors themselves. In general, people like to talk about what they do. Interviews should be direct, tactful, and time limited. To be sure, not all the information one would like to have will be obtained, but a good deal will be.

Researchers must marshal the data they collect in order to answer the following representative market-research questions:

- What is the *specific* business I want to enter? Is it for all potential conference center consumers or just, say, for senior corporate executives? Or for fellow nonprofit executives? Or perhaps a center just for the disabled?

- Is the market niche clear?

- Is it viable? Is the marketplace large enough and fluid enough to accommodate a new player?

- Is the market for conference centers growing, stable, or contracting? Which customer segments provide what proportion of sales in the business? What are the long-term prospects for growth?

- Is market entry easy? Is it costly? What grade of facilities and what amenities are crucial to attracting a share of the marketplace? What capital improvements will be needed to enter the marketplace?

- Who is the competition? How entrenched is it? How do they market and sell their services? What are their prices and profit margins?

- How does the business market its services? Who are the people that must be attracted to buy—directors of training? vice-presidents for human resources? CEOs?

- Does the business rise and fall with inclement weather? Seasonally? Are there geographical factors that affect the success of the operation?

- Are there particular labor issues likely to cause problems? Is unionization a factor? Can part-time staff be used and are they available?

- How long will it take to get the facility up and running? How far in advance are conferences booked? What kind of marketing is necessary to attract the targeted market? How costly is marketing?

This list of questions, by no means exhaustive, lies at the heart of the research. Yet the answers—complete answers—are still of limited utility. They will have meaning to the organization only when measured against the results of the internal audit. Successful entrepreneurial ventures result when thorough, high quality market analysis matches the internal capability to execute the findings.

Nonprofits can discern market opportunities that are outstanding, yet be so internally weak and disorganized that the likelihood of success is minimal. Other nonprofits may be internally strong and capable of starting an earned income venture, only to find their market research reveals a venture of only marginal possibilities. *Both* findings must be strongly positive in order to proceed.

What kind of internal questions need to be answered? They are the ones that grow out of the internal audit, which the organization has performed earlier. Some of them are:

- Does the venture fit comfortably within the exempt mission of our organization?
- Will our funders, staff members, contributors, and clients look favorably on it?
- Do our trustees support the venture?
- Do we have enough staff to plan for and execute the venture?
- Is our financial condition strong enough to try this venture? Is our long-term support assured? Will other programs suffer from this new activity?
- Does our management (especially our chief executive officer) have the depth and expertise to carry off the venture?

The market research phase is an extensive one and could involve several months and numerous staff people. At its conclusion, a written report should be prepared, describing the findings of the research and recommending specific actions to the executive director and the board of trustees.

THE FEASIBILITY STUDY

At this point the organization is perhaps a third of the way down the funnel. The channeling process has helped surface and then select a variety of entrepreneurial options. The feasibility study fills in at least three areas covered only partially in the market research: specifics about marketing the product or service, a discussion of the organization of the business, and a statement about the financial nature of the business.

The feasibility study is a formal investigation of a venture. It clearly defines the opportunities and the risks to the organization if it decides to enter a business. It is usually done from a skeptical point of view, from the vantage point of why the idea can *not* work. It is designed to reveal any "yellow blinking lights" on the road to the venture start-up.

Marketing

Based on the market research, the organization should delve further into how the product or service is commonly marketed, and what the organization can do to match or improve upon the usual approach. For example, some products are introduced by large amounts of advertising; others succeed by word of mouth. Some products and services are marketed with premiums or special introductory prices to attract customers; others are priced high and kept scarce. Some are focused on a limited geographical area; others reach for the largest possible audience. Some are sold directly through salespersons, others through direct mail, and still others through passive displays in prominent locations. This phase of marketing scopes out the specific marketing channels and approaches and offers a sense of the workload needed to accomplish the task.

Organization

Some businesses are military and vertical, while others are more flexible and horizontal. The feasibility study fills in how similar businesses are conducted and managed, through start-up and post-start-up phases. It lists the types of positions that need to be filled, and reporting relationships and the kinds of overhead support important to success. The study does not include names of persons who might be employed in the business, or their positions, or their specific responsibilities. It is a skeleton, which accurately depicts the way the business should be organized.

Finances

The financial analysis gives an accurate profile of similar businesses in the field, the size of the investment that may be needed for the venture, profitability ratios of similar ventures (if it is running well), and rough expense breakdowns. It reveals how close or far away the analyst is from having the capital to start and prevail in the venture. It does not describe how this particular business would be run, or its revenue, expenses, profits, and losses.

All markets change and some change more rapidly than others. A feasibility study must be based on the most up-to-date statistics and constantly be rewritten to reflect changes in the marketplace. Accordingly, the study should be done with some dispatch. It is not the job for a part-time intern or a distracted executive director. It is not uncommon for the study to take three to six months.

The feasibility study will conclude in a formal written report recommending a go- or no-go decision. It should persuade the chief executive officer and board members that this is *the* business for the organization. If they approve, the nonprofit has taken a long step forward toward producing the final document, the business plan.

A review of the steps that precede the business plan makes clear that enterprise cannot be taken lightly, no matter how much of a "winner" the organization is convinced it has. Every step is taken for a reason, with appropriate resources devoted to meet the particular task. Since many nonprofits exist in chronically scarce environments, they need to constantly trade off opportunities to achieve their charitable end. An earned income activity can become a competitor for scarce resources and, accordingly, must be analyzed both on its own terms and within the context of the charitable programs of the organization. Because enterprise can threaten the financial stability of the entire operation, and jeopardize the capability of the organization to perform its exempt mission, it should be undertaken with deliberation and skill.

The process of venture analysis may also have a side benefit—a better understanding of the way the organization functions and how its staff communicate. Exercises such as feasibility studies can tell senior executives a good deal about their operations, not only whether an earned income activity might fit comfortably within the nonprofit, but also how healthy are the organization's communication patterns, morale, and working environment.

4

Planning and Implementing Marketing Programs in Nonprofit Organizations

CHRISTOPHER H. LOVELOCK and CHARLES B. WEINBERG

MARKETING CAN PLAY A PIVOTAL ROLE in improving management practice and increasing earned income of nonprofit organizations. As a broad strategic function that permeates the organization, marketing helps link the organization to its external environments—its customers, funding sources, competitors, regulatory agencies, and other relevant publics.

This chapter offers a framework for looking at marketing issues and for developing and implementing marketing strategies. The emphasis is on the current state of the art within nonprofit organizations and how it can be improved.

Historically, the marketing discipline concerned itself with physical goods produced by the private sector. Not until the mid-1970s were concerted efforts made by the public and nonprofit sectors to learn more about marketing and its applications. Indeed, until quite recently, many nonprofit administrators resisted the very notion of marketing. They regarded the concept as inappropriate for their type of organization. They felt the terminology was unseemly and arcane, and they saw the actual practice of marketing strategies as positively unethical.

At the other end of the spectrum were a smaller number of managers who embraced marketing with more enthusiasm than understanding. It was almost as if marketing were a magic wand that, if waved by the right professional wizard, would transform an unloved institution into a Cinderella princess. Since miracles rarely

Copyright © 1988 by Christopher H. Lovelock and Charles B. Weinberg.

This chapter is based in part on *Marketing for Public and Nonprofit Managers* by Christopher H. Lovelock and Charles B. Weinberg, second edition (Redwood City, CA: The Scientific Press, 1988). The helpful comments of Gerald Gorn and Richard Pollay are gratefully acknowledged.

happen in marketing, these individuals were usually disappointed and frequently disillusioned.

A third group of nonprofit managers felt immediately at home with the basic philosophy of marketing, since it was akin to their existing approach to management. They recognized that it made sense to understand the needs and concerns of one's users or clients. They developed programs *targeted at specific groups,* tailoring delivery systems, prices—if any—and communication to the characteristics of these groups. These managers looked at other organizations to see if they were offering similar or substitute services to the same target group and, if so, how to adapt or respond. They developed plans to achieve well-defined goals. They coordinated all programmatic activities to ensure consistency, leveraged efforts through third parties (e.g., by conducting blood drives through corporate personnel departments) when this resulted in greater effectiveness or lower costs, evaluated program performance on an ongoing basis, and modified the program and its execution in the light of this evaluation. This disciplined approach is characteristic of successful marketing practice in nonprofit organizations.

DISTINCTIVE CHARACTERISTICS OF NONPROFIT MARKETING

Dominance of Nonfinancial Objective

By definition, nonprofit organizations do not seek to make a profit for redistribution to owners or shareholders. Because most nonbusiness organizations neither seek a financial surplus nor expect operating revenues to cover full costs, their mission invariably gives priority to nonfinancial objectives. The primary "bottom line" for nonbusiness entities is thus some form of "social profit."

This objective makes it hard to measure success or failure in strictly financial terms. How can we tell if one university or nonprofit hospital is more successful than another, or if the children's museum in city X is better than that in city Y? More difficult still, how can we compare the performance of a university to a hospital, or to a museum? Successes in fund raising or in obtaining customers can be measured and compared, but these are means to an end, not an end in themselves.

From a strictly marketing standpoint, the absence of even a theoretical goal of financial profitability makes it harder for managers to set objectives, to choose among strategic and tactical alternatives, and to evaluate performance after the fact. The problem is at its toughest when no monetary price is charged for the organization's product. When consumers do make a direct payment, sales-revenue goals can be set and performance measured in terms of the proportion of total and incremental costs covered by customer-derived revenues.

Any shortfall between sales revenues and costs must, of course, be made up by voluntary donations or other subsidies. The justification for either is that the social profit generated by the organization matches or exceeds the financial cost of obtaining it. This notion requires development of nonfinancial measures (for example, wilderness areas preserved and attitudes changed by a conservation society) that can be used to document performance.

Need for Resource Attraction

All organizations need resources to function. Business firms expect to pay for the resources they use—labor, materials, land, and expertise. Nonprofit organizations are sometimes able to get these resources for free (volunteered labor, services in kind, donated facilities, exemption from property taxes), or at a reduced rate (discounted postal rates, tax concessions, and so forth). Moreover, while most businesses seek funds from the financial markets to underwrite research and development, working capital, and expansion, they ultimately expect sales revenue to exceed costs. By contrast, the vast majority of nonprofit organizations cannot cover costs from sales revenues and must devote continuing efforts to seeking new donations and grants or to preserving the flow of such revenues from existing sources.

Nonprofit marketers, then, are dealing with two interrelated marketing tasks, not one. The first involves programs to *attract* needed resources; the second involves programs to *allocate* these resources in pursuit of the organizational mission.

Multiple Constituencies

The need to engage in both resource attraction and resource allocation activities means that nonprofit executives must deal with two sets of "customers." Balancing the needs and expectations of both groups can sometimes be difficult. For example, some donors may demand that money be used to serve a population group or to supply a type of product different from those that management feels are most appropriate. Often, the result is unsatisfactory. Some arts groups, for instance, have felt compelled by terms of government grants to attract a populist audience for whom their performances are not designed.

The number of constituencies faced by nonprofit organizations is often increased by the presence of third-party payers (such as health insurance firms or parents who pay college tuition for their children), politicians and regulatory agencies, former consumers (such as college alumni) with a continuing interest in the performance of "their" institution, and the mass media. Few business managers have to juggle the interests of as many constituencies as do their nonprofit counterparts.

Tension Between Mission and Customer Satisfaction

A basic tenet of marketing suggests that organizations will do best if they are attentive to their customers' needs and wants. While not all companies adhere rigorously to a philosophy of "the customer is always right," most do seek to satisfy consumer needs. This model breaks down in the case of nonprofit organizations, where consumer sovereignty may sometimes be seen as alien to fulfillment of the institutional mission.

For example, the mission of nonprofit organizations often requires them to take a long-term view rather than pander to current popular tastes. Medical treatments must consider the long-term needs of the patient, not how he or she would like to feel or act tomorrow. Religious organizations have a spiritual mission to fulfill, often involving self-sacrifice. A university seeks to transmit skills, knowledge, and ways of thinking and reasoning that will have extended value to students—not simply to amuse and inspire them for the duration of the course in question. And many arts organizations believe they have a mission to educate their patrons to appreciate new art forms. The tension is not always adjusted smoothly. Many nonprofits are in constant conflict over the interpretation of their mission by various constituencies and these tensions are exacerbated in a resource-scarce environment.

Ability to Obtain Free or Inexpensive Support

In conducting their marketing efforts, managers of nonprofit organizations are often able to draw on donated labor and services. For example, the United Way and its member agencies receive millions of dollars worth of free advertising time during televised professional football games. As another example, volunteers play key roles in helping universities raise money from their alumni, in providing nonmedical services to hospital patients, in operating retail stores in museums, and in serving as guides at many historic properties.

These benefits can compensate for some of the disadvantages under which nonprofit managers must frequently operate. Wisely sought and carefully used, they can provide a powerful way to stretch resources. Nevertheless, free or discounted resources need strong (yet sensitive) management, perhaps even more so than those purchased at market prices. For example, a museum shop is likely to be unsuccessful if its volunteer sales clerks have high absenteeism rates and do not acquire needed selling skills and product knowledge.

Management in Duplicate or Triplicate

A final factor distinguishing nonprofit marketing programs from those in the private sector concerns the large number of fingers in the managerial pie. In many nonprofit enterprises, trustees or directors assume management responsibilities, and volunteers occupy places in the management hierarchy. Such individuals seldom have direct reporting relationships with the paid administrative staff. They can be a help or a hindrance, and sometimes both.

The problems of "duplicate management" are compounded in situations where the service is planned and delivered by professionals who outrank the managers responsible for running the operation. In the arts, higher education, and health care, disputes often arise between management personnel on the one hand, and administrators/professionals such as curators, faculty members, and doctors on the other. Professionals, such as faculty members in a college, are typically both the producers of the organization's product and possess considerable expertise in their chosen fields. It is not surprising then that professionals have not always been willing to accept the introduction of a strong user orientation that suggests that outsiders may know more about a service, or at least certain aspects of it, than the professionals.

MARKET AND CONSUMER ANALYSIS

Marketing is concerned with the process by which people adopt and maintain attitudes and behavior patterns. Marketing managers seek to understand potential or actual consumers in order to influence their behavior. For example, in the context of a theater, a marketing manager wants to know how a person decides to go to a theater, the alternatives considered, the relative importance of social, educational, and financial factors, and how often the person now attends performances. Many managers find that they must not only consider individuals, but also the decision-making processes of whole families, institutions, regulatory bodies, and other groups. Information is then needed on both the formal and informal influence and decision processes in such groups.

Needed information can sometimes come from existing (secondary) sources, such as published studies or internal records within the organization. At other times, new (primary) research may be needed to obtain the desired information. *Market research* is an essential tool—for planning, performance monitoring, and the evaluation of marketing programs. Few successful marketing programs are implemented or sustainable without an underlying base of market research.

Market research involves a sequence of steps, termed the research process, as summarized in Table I. When a study is begun, it may be tempting to go straight to

---

TABLE I. MARKET RESEARCH PROCESS

Purpose of research: Why is information to be gathered?

Statement of research objectives: What information is needed?

Review of existing data: What is already known?

Value analysis: Is the research worth the cost?

Research design: How are the data to be collected?
  Exploratory studies (e.g., focus groups)
  Descriptive (e.g., surveys)
  Causal (e.g., field experiments)

Research tactics
  Data collection method (personal or telephone interview, mail survey, observation)
  Definition of target population
  Sample selection and size
  Instrument design
  Pretesting

Field operations: Actual collection of the data

Data analysis

Completing the project
  Interpreting the data
  Recommendations
  Report writing

---

instrument design and data collection, with not enough thought given to the prior steps. This is a serious mistake and often leads to market-research reports that are not useful because the wrong questions were asked or the data collected turn out to be unreliable and inaccurate. Successful market research requires a systematic approach to data collection, so that enough information will be provided to influence policy and to help managers make decisions.

Market Segmentation

Most marketing organizations find themselves operating in mass markets of thousands or even millions of customers and prospective customers. How can managers—especially nonprofit managers—reconcile the need to be attentive to the concerns of individual consumers with the need to run an efficient operation, which tends to dictate undifferentiated treatment of large numbers of customers?

One approach lies in *market segmentation*—the development and pursuit of marketing programs directed at specific, differentiated groups the organization could potentially serve. Segmentation serves two basic managerial purposes. The first is *market definition,* i.e., helping an organization to identify and select those segments that are most closely related to fulfillment of institutional objectives. The second is *target marketing,* i.e., helping managers develop and implement finely tuned strategies designed to meet the needs of their chosen segments. This may require making further subdivisions in the target population and coordinating several marketing programs tailored to each of them. A segmentation strategy also provides a clearer focus for the organization and for the people who manage and work in that enterprise.

Market segmentation can also help nonprofit organizations in attracting funds from donors and government agencies. A clear specification of market targets and institutional mission allows an organization to identify the donor segments that are most likely to be responsive to fund-raising appeals. An obvious illustration is the science museum that seeks donations from high technology firms.

Moreover, a segmentation strategy can assist management in reducing the impact of competition by focusing on a particular population group not well served. For instance, Hood College, a liberal-arts college for women, elected to remain a single-sex institution in the middle 1970s, at a time when many women's colleges felt that they could compete more effectively by becoming coeducational. Hood succeeded in establishing a leadership role for itself among the declining number of women's colleges, attracting female students who preferred this concept of education.

Some barriers exist to using market segmentation strategies in nonprofit organizations. Unlike their private-sector counterparts, managers of nonprofit organizations may not have the luxury of picking and choosing the segments they would like to serve. They may be constrained by their charter, their historical record, their constituencies, or their funding. They may be narrowly constrained to certain segments or given such a broad mandate that activities cannot be focused tightly. Sometimes managers face strong opposition from traditionally minded donors, trustees, existing users, and other relevant supporters if they attempt to extend their current services or efforts to appeal to new segments.

Market segmentation is a great improvement over undifferentiated mass marketing. It requires an organization to be focused and not to be all things to all people. The concept of market segmentation is based on three propositions: 1) consumers are different, 2) differences in consumers are related to differences in market behavior, and 3) segments of consumers can be isolated within the overall market. With successful market segmentation, management can do its job more efficiently and effectively.

ELEMENTS OF THE MARKETING MIX

The execution of a marketing strategy requires the use of a broad array of marketing tools. Decisions must be made in four major areas, collectively referred to as the *marketing mix*. These are: 1) the characteristics of the *product* that is offered in the marketplace; 2) the *price* that is charged—including the dollar amount and how it is to be paid for, as well as nonfinancial costs; 3) *distribution*—where, when, and how the goods and services are delivered; and 4) *communication*—which involves developing the messages directed at prospective markets, as well as choosing the means by which these messages are transmitted. The interdependence among these four elements requires that marketing managers understand the role played by each in the marketing mix and ensure that the total strategy is consistent and meets the organization's goals efficiently.

Product

The output of nonprofit organizations varies enormously. Most produce services, ranging from health care to higher education, from the visual arts to the performing arts. Others market causes or social-behavior patterns with goals ranging from saving sea mammals to saving souls, from banning handguns to banning abortion. A few even produce goods as their primary activity, and a growing number are starting to market physical goods as a profit-making sideline. The term *products* is used generically in this chapter to refer to the goods or services offered or behaviors advocated by an organization.

The nonprofit organization must make two critical decisions: *which products* to offer and, as already discussed, *which market segments* to target. All other strategic marketing-mix decisions flow from these decisions. Pricing, distribution, and communication are facilitating tools in a marketing program—not the driving force behind it.

Many nonprofit organizations, especially in the service sector, view their products from a different perspective than do prospective customers. The service provider usually considers the product to be much more important than the user does. For instance, while highway safety organizations view wearing seat belts as vital, the great majority of the population is indifferent to this behavior. Management must avoid thinking that what they do (or sell) is either indispensible or morally compelling. It is the marketplace that determines a product's acceptance, and the motivation to purchase derives from the benefits that the customer expects to receive.

Viewed in this way, a product is a bundle of benefits that customers obtain in exchange for an investment of their money, time, and, perhaps, a certain amount of hassle. Moreover, not all individuals (or institutional purchasers) necessarily seek the same benefits. Hence it may be appropriate to develop alternative versions of the same overall product to appeal to different segments within the market, and to market that product differently. For instance, an art museum might have school groups tour areas of the museum containing exhibits likely to appeal to teenagers, while special library and research facilities are reserved for art historians. As another example, the alcoholism treatment program designed for a young, unattached individual likely differs from one designed for middle-aged executives, who have families to provide emotional support.

Most nonprofit organizations offer products that can be grouped into three categories: 1) core products tied directly to the institutional mission, 2) supplementary products (e.g., film or lecture programs at a museum) that facilitate or enhance customers' use of the core product(s), and 3) resource-attraction products (e.g., bingo games in church halls) that help draw the financing needed to run the organization where the revenues derived from core and supplementary products are insufficient to cover operating outlays.

Organizations offering multiple products must think in terms of their *product portfolio*, and not simply examine each product in isolation. They must choose which ones to emphasize in a marketing strategy. They should evaluate each product simultaneously against two criteria: 1) the net financial contribution it makes, and 2) its ability to advance the institutional mission. Supplementary services, such as a university bookstore, are sometimes constrained to neither make a profit (in fairness to the students who are a captive market) nor a loss (to avoid imposing a drain on organizational funds). Because many core products lose money (even after allocating earmarked grants and donations), resource-attraction products (such as sale of gifts or rental of facilities for social functions) may be needed to cover the deficit.

Changes in the nonprofit organization's environment may require adjustments to the product portfolio. Videotapes may displace books as a teaching tool, or a Spanish-speaking majority may demand a new approach to literacy programming. Whole neighborhoods may shift character, isolating or negating the appeal of a cultural program to the local area. Some existing products may have to be dropped; they may have reached the end of their life cycle and are outmoded and unprofitable, or perhaps they no longer advance the institutional mission in useful ways. Sometimes, redesigning and repositioning the product may be a feasible option. In response to medical progress, the March of Dimes has changed its focus from polio to birth defects and the American Lung Association from tuberculosis (which has become a minor disease) to emphysema, lung cancer, and asthma. Consideration should also be given to the identification, development, and introduction of new products—a process requiring rigorous evaluation of possible alternatives and careful attention to detail.

Pricing Strategies

When marketing managers ask themselves, "How much shall we charge?" and consumers inquire, "How much does it cost?" both groups probably have in mind the monetary price of the product. However, customers consider other costs when presented with an organization's offering. For one thing, time is a precious commodity, one whose supply for each individual has a fixed upper limit. There is an opportunity cost to the time spent traveling and waiting in pursuit of a service, or in trying to behave in ways urged by a social marketer. There may also be psychic costs attached to the use of a particular service—feelings of discomfort, inferiority, social disapproval from others, or even fear. Family-planning clinics, as well as other counseling services, need to pay particular attention to such feelings. In short, the bundle of benefits presented by the product must be traded off against the bundle of costs associated with using it. These nonmonetary prices assume greater prominence in the case of free or low-cost services, where one might at first assume there would be no barriers to access at all.

Costs, competition, and market demand are the foundations of a pricing strategy. The costs to be recovered set a floor to the price that may be charged; the value of the product to the customer sets a ceiling; and the price charged by competitors for similar or substitute products may determine where, within the ceiling-to-floor range, the price level should actually be set.

The pricing-strategy principles of the private sector have to be modified for nonprofit organizations. Companies must recover the full costs associated with producing and marketing a product, and then charge a sufficient margin on top to yield a satisfactory profit. In a nonprofit organization, by contrast, donations often cover a significant portion of the costs, thus reducing the amount to be recovered through price. Many nonprofit organizations are unwilling to charge the maximum level that consumers might be willing to pay—even in situations where private-sector competitors are successfully doing so—since the institutional mission may require that the product be made available to prospective customers inexpensively, or even free of charge. Many community centers offer fitness programs and swimming lessons at prices well below those of private health clubs.

The image desired by the organization may also influence pricing strategy. For instance, the American Repertory Theatre in Boston surveyed the prices charged by competing theaters in the Boston area to help it in setting prices for its own performances. The A.R.T. management felt that it was important to have a top price "high enough to distinguish us from the church basement productions . . . but on the other hand, we do depend on outside funding and for that reason we can't be out for blood like the commercial theatres."[1]

---

[1] Penny Pittman Merliss and Christopher H. Lovelock, "American Repertory Theatre" in Christopher H. Lovelock and Charles B. Weinberg, *Public and Nonprofit Marketing: Cases and Readings*, Redwood City, CA: The Scientific Press, 1984, p. 250.

Prospective customers can often be segmented according to their ability and willingness to pay. The challenge for marketing managers is to determine the price sensitivity of each segment and to devise ways of charging customers in each segment a price that reflects their differential ability to pay. Nonprofit marketers may sometimes find themselves constrained by public expectations of a "fair" price. Similarly, they may be accused of discrimination if different segments are charged widely varying prices for what is perceived as the "same" service.

Occasionally, nonprofit organizations compete with private firms. On rare occasions, but, it would appear, increasingly, these businesses claim unfair competition when they feel that such agencies are pricing services below their true cost. Libraries, which traditionally provide service at no charge, are now struggling to set appropriate prices for computer-based and other information-search services for which private firms charge substantial fees.

A realistic decision on pricing is critical for the financial solvency of the organization. As shown in Table II, many factors need to be considered in setting price. Beyond the amount itself, a variety of other pricing issues must be considered when developing a pricing policy, including the use of financing or service intermediaries and availability of credit.

Distribution and Delivery Systems

Distribution is concerned with making desired goods and services available to consumers in a location and at a time that is convenient—the right product, at the right time, in the right place. Because the products of nonprofit organizations are predominantly services, the design of the service delivery system assumes particular importance. In many instances, consumption takes place at the site of the service provider and is simultaneous with final production of the service. Thus the site itself and the manner of delivering a service can influence the way consumers see the product and their satisfaction with it. Success requires that management coordinate activities from both an operations (or production) standpoint and a marketing (or user) viewpoint.

A service provider needs to be more concerned than a manufacturer with the characteristics of the site where service is provided. Site characteristics include: geographic location, accessibility, manner of providing service, service personnel, physical appearance, and operating hours. The last is a particular concern because many services are "perishable" and cannot be stored for later use. Thus an orchestra cannot use its performance on Tuesday night to satisfy audience members who wish to attend a live concert on Saturday night, and a transit system's excess capacity at midday does not relieve congestion during the commuting hours.

The geographically dispersed nature of the distribution system makes quality control a difficult problem. Moreover, the fact that services are delivered by personnel (employees or volunteers) who do not always act in a consistent manner heightens the difficulty of setting performance standards and ensuring their fulfillment. As users generally place a high value on reliable, consistent service, this area deserves serious management attention. Training programs, operating manuals, and control systems

TABLE II. SOME PRICING ISSUES

How Much Should Be Charged for This Product?
What costs is the organization attempting to recover?
Is the organization trying to achieve a surplus by selling this product?
How do consumer segments react to different prices?
Does donor or government support depend on the prices charged?
How sensitive are customers to different prices?
What prices are charged by competitors?
What discount(s) should Be offered from basic prices?
Are psychological pricing points (e.g., $4.95 versus $5.00) customarily used?

Who Should Collect Payment?
The organization that provides the service
A specialist intermediary (e.g., travel or ticket agent, bank, retailer, etc.)

Where Should Prices Be Paid?
The location at which the product is delivered
A convenient retail outlet or financial intermediary (e.g., bank)
The purchaser's home (by mail or phone)

When Should Prices Be Paid?
Before or after delivery of the product?
At which times of day?
On which days of the week?

How Should Prices Be Paid?
Cash (exact change or not?), check, or credit card?
Loan from financial intermediary
Vouchers
Third-party payment (e.g., insurance company, government agency)

How Should Prices Be Communicated to the Target Market?
Communication media
Message content (how much emphasis should be placed on price?)
Timing of messages

that emphasize customer service standards are three approaches to this problem; but, for these to be effective, a consumer orientation must first be developed throughout the organization.

Nonprofit managers cannot afford to overlook distribution and service-delivery issues. For example, hospitals in the United States must confront a sharp decline in inpatient days of care and increased competition from new health delivery systems, such as health maintenance organizations (HMOs) and freestanding (physically apart from a hospital) emergency care facilities. In response, some hospitals have adopted approaches to distributing health care services, such as: 1) expanding the number of sites at which a hospital provides some of its services, 2) increasing geographic market coverage by providing transportation services, and 3) vertically integrating by developing special relationships with doctors and health clinics.

Marketing Communication

Communication is the most visible or audible—some would say intrusive—of marketing activities. An old marketing axiom says that the fastest way to kill a poor product is to advertise it heavily. Conversely, an otherwise well planned marketing strategy, designed to deliver, say, counseling on family planning at a reasonable price, and at times and locations tailored to consumer needs, is likely to fail if people lack knowledge of the service.

Through communication, the marketer can inform existing or prospective customers about product, price, and distribution details; create (where appropriate) persuasive arguments for using the service, buying the product, or adopting the recommended social behavior; and remind people of the product—especially at times and in locations where purchase is particularly relevant.

The four broad categories of marketing communication are: 1) personal selling, 2) media advertising, 3) publicity and public relations, and 4) promotional or informational activities at the point of sale. These four categories are well known, although managers frequently emphasize media advertising and personal selling over the others. Moreover, some executives do not recognize the many other ways in which an organization communicates with its customers. The appearance of a physical product or of service personnel, the way a customer is treated, the price charged, the location and atmosphere of a service delivery facility—all contribute to a general impression that reinforces or contradicts the impression created by specific messages. For example, a social service agency may spend many hours and a good deal of money developing an advertising campaign built around the message "We care"; but a single rude or indifferent receptionist at the agency can shatter that image in an instant.

For many nonprofit marketers, political or financial restrictions may constrain their ability to engage in expensive communication efforts. For others, the fear of spending money on communication restricts their efforts. In both cases, they may be condemning their organizations to operating far below their potential—and even risking failure in the process. Another group of managers, while reluctant to spend money, does recognize the need to inform customers about their products. The latter's approach is to seek out sources of "free" communication, such as public service advertising, public relations activities, and volunteer salespeople. For some organizations, this works well; for others, it may represent a false economy. The key problem of relying on donated services is the potential loss of control over message content, format, and scheduling that may result.

COMPETITIVE POSTURE AND POSITIONING STRATEGY

Competition has traditionally been associated with the private sector. Nonprofit organizations were typically formed to provide services that high-minded citizens believed to be desirable for society but where a profit was seen either as inappropriate to its mission or as an unattainable objective. Consequently, few of the longer established nonprofit organizations were conceived with competition in mind. Most met an established demand that was insufficient, at the prices prevailing, to attract profit-seeking competitors. Yet, over time, as the environment has changed, a competitive posture has become necessary for survival.

There are several reasons for this situation. In some instances, as in higher education, demand has shrunk relative to supply, so institutions that once peacefully coexisted are now fighting among themselves for a larger share of a shrinking pie. In other instances, exemplified by hospitals, the private sector has seemingly chosen to focus on certain segments of the population with a subset of services that can be offered at a profit. Changes in both technology and consumer needs, as well as the availability of third-party payments, have resulted in an upsurge in generic competition. New products—both goods and services—offered by the private sector compete with products once available only from the public or nonprofit sectors. The field of library information services, fueled by the growth of computer-based data sources, is one example already mentioned.

Finally, in an effort to make better use of their existing resources and skills, and to provide a financial contribution toward operating overheads, many nonprofit organizations have added to their existing "product lines" new goods and services that are potentially profitable. Some compete directly with private sector offerings. Examples include retail shops, printed materials (e.g., calendars from the Sierra Club), educational programs, vacation activities (e.g., historical tours hosted by university professors), and so forth.

To this litany of new competitive factors, perhaps we should also add the tightened market—relative to demand—for government funding, philanthropic donations, and volunteers' time.

Competition is not limited to organizations that offer similar goods and services; it can be indirect as well. "Generic" competition can come from organizations offering different products but similar benefits to consumers. For example, there may only be one symphony orchestra in a city, but many potential audience members would consider the opera, ballet, and the theater acceptable alternative ways to spend an evening.

An organization should examine its position as compared to the competition to see how the market perceives and desires its offerings. Some organizations may find that the market perceives only minimal distinctions between offerings. For example, in one such instance, a community center offering preschool day care programs thought that it was differentiated in the marketplace because of its religious affiliation and content. However, a survey of parents showed that this affiliation made little difference. Parents felt that five or six local day care centers were roughly equivalent on all important service dimensions. They therefore chose on the basis of price and location.

Some organizations are perceived as being relatively distinctive. To continue the day care example, parents believed that one preschool program in the area had a particularly effective educational program and consequently positioned that organization separately. It attracted children from a wider geographic radius and at higher fees than did any of the other schools. By developing a unique competitive position, this center prospered while others were barely surviving.

Adjustment to competitive realities is often a difficult task for nonprofit managers. Central to developing a competitive posture is understanding the concept of *positioning*.

A positioning strategy involves: 1) selecting target-market segments on which to concentrate, 2) identifying the positions held by competitive offerings in the relevant markets, and 3) choosing a position that is (currently or potentially) important to the relevant markets. Positioning brings together market analysis, internal analysis of organizational resources and constraints, and competitive analysis. Once chosen, a positioning strategy forms the framework on which to build the elements of the marketing mix. The product, pricing, and distribution elements create the chosen position, while communication efforts convey this position to the relevant target market.

In short, positioning is the process of establishing and maintaining a distinctive place in the market. This applies to an entire organization and/or its product offerings. A position is held with respect to performance on specific characteristics. In a competitive marketplace it is usually related to the positions held by competing products or organizations. Thus, a hospital that stresses its emergency services for patients may seek the image of a well-equipped, quick-response health care center—a different position from one sought by a hospital that specializes in the latest techniques of heart surgery and appeals to an international market of patients referred by physicians practicing on several continents. Of course, the position held by an organization should be consistent with its basic mission and purposes.

Positioning analysis provides a diagnostic tool to help an organization understand the relationship between its products and the markets it serves. The analysis can suggest where new opportunities lie through either developing new products or repositioning existing ones. An organization should choose for itself the position it wishes to occupy; if it postpones or avoids positioning, the market or competition may force it into an unappealing stance. A nonprofit counseling service for women entering the labor force needs to avoid being positioned as being suitable only for women with limited job-related skills.

BUILDING A MARKETING PLAN

A well-chosen positioning strategy provides the foundation for the formulation of a coordinated, consistent *marketing plan*. The marketing plan is a systematic way of organizing an analysis of a market, an organization's position in that market, and a program for future marketing activities. All marketing strategies depend on and should be related to such analysis.

The elements of a marketing plan are not discrete; they are interrelated, so that developing a plan may involve cycling through its components several times before satisfactory results are achieved. Table III lists important issues that should be included in a marketing plan.

Particularly for organizations new to marketing, a useful precursor to developing a marketing plan is conducting a *marketing audit*, as shown in Figure 1. A marketing audit is a carefully programmed procedure for carrying out a broad, objective review

TABLE III. MARKETING PLAN FORMAT

Executive Summary

Situational analysis (Where are we now?)
  External
  Environment (political, regulatory, economic, social, technical, etc.)
    Consumers
    Employees
    Funders
    Distributors
    Competition
  Internal
    Objectives
    Strengths and weaknesses

Problems and opportunities

Marketing program goals (Where do we want to go?)
  Specific (quantifiable)
  Realistic (attainable)
  Important
  Prioritized

Marketing strategies (How are we going to get there?)
  Positioning
    Target segments
    Competitive stance
    Usage incentive
  Marketing mix
    Product
    Price
    Distribution
    Marketing communication
  Contingency strategies

Marketing budget (How much and where?)
  Resources
    Money
    People
    Time
  Amount and allocation

Marketing action plan
  Detailed breakdown of activities for each goal or strategy
  Responsibility by name
  Activity schedule in milestone format
  Tangible and intangible results expected from each activity

Monitoring system

FIGURE 1. A MARKETING AUDIT STRUCTURE

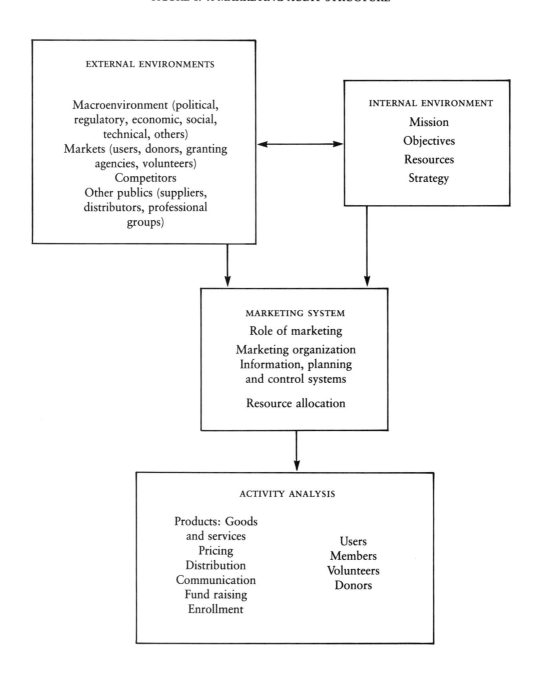

and appraisal of an organization's marketing strategy and performance. Its use in both the business and the nonprofit sectors is on the increase. While managers often review and appraise the effectiveness of such individual marketing activities as advertising programs, the product line, and fund-raising campaigns, they usually evaluate each element separately and at a different time. In contrast, a marketing audit provides an integrated appraisal encompassing a broad range of marketing issues. An audit can cover the organization's external environment, internal environment, marketing systems, and marketing activities. Besides being a diagnostic tool in which weaknesses in the current marketing structure are uncovered, the marketing audit can reveal both future threats and opportunities and be a source of recommendations for change. The marketing audit therefore helps to identify opportunities and the means to exploit them.

IMPLEMENTING MARKETING PROGRAMS

Implementation should not be separated from such other managerial tasks as analysis, planning, and decision making. Success requires that all aspects of management be integrated; the strategy formed at one level of the organization needs to be implemented at lower levels. This cascading effect of strategy and tactics extends throughout the organization. To illustrate this point, a community center's strategic decision to serve teenagers can be effective only if there are program personnel to design meaningful, attractive programs. In turn, these programs are worth little unless the community center's workers can actually perform the program's requirements. Strategy and implementation form a cycle, each affecting the other.

A critical task for newly appointed marketing managers in an organization that has previously lacked a formal marketing function is to choose appropriate early assignments; they should look for projects that are seen as useful by other managers, have reasonable visibility, and offer a high chance of success in a relatively short time period. One community college manager's first marketing program successfully boosted enrollment in satellite campuses, an area that had been largely overlooked by administrators concentrating on the main campus. One advantage of working for an organization that has neglected marketing is that there are usually a number of such projects available. Rescheduling classes to better meet the needs of part-time students, preparing more effective and honest catalogs, and revitalizing the bookstore were but three areas available for substantial improvement. Instigators of marketing should recognize that initial projects are only that; these pioneering managers must continue to develop the utilization of marketing until it is fully accepted as a vital, necessary, and ongoing organizational activity. Marketing's role is more than just to provide a means of remedying present difficulties and carrying out specific projects; it serves a proactive function that helps an organization to anticipate future events and initiate actions allowing it to succeed in a changing environment.

Successfully completed early projects, in addition to being necessary and useful themselves, also represent building blocks toward the establishment of a formal marketing function. For marketing to become a permanent part of the organization, two conditions are necessary: 1) support from the chief executive officer (CEO) of the organization, and 2) establishment of a senior executive with responsibility for marketing.

Without support of the CEO, marketing cannot become a significant strategic function. Marketing introduces the reality and complexity of a dynamic, competitive environment into an organization's planning and operations. As such, it appears to make the job of the other management functions more difficult—although in the long run, a marketing orientation makes the organization more responsive, vital, and successful. For example, the task of financial management is made more difficult because substantial expenditures are often required to develop and plan marketing programs. Investments must often be made in intangibles, such as marketing research, service development, and personnel training, the value of which does not appear on the balance sheet along with physical assets. Given support from the CEO, the placement of a senior executive with marketing responsibility at high levels of the organization allows marketing to have an impact on management equal to that of the other major functional areas. Performing arts organizations and hospitals are two examples of nonprofit fields that have seen the growth of senior executive positions in marketing.

Implementation of marketing means more than just developing marketing plans and assigning responsibility for them to specific individuals. It also includes examining its role in the overall organization, facilitating its interaction with other functional areas of management, and developing a strong consumer orientation throughout the institution. In particular, the necessity of reconciling marketing and operations viewpoints must be stressed. A key area is the customer-contact function. Personnel in direct contact with users have to reflect a customer orientation at the same time that they participate in the production of the agency's service. For too long, nonprofit organizations have been dominated by an operations orientation focused on creating and delivering a service in an operationally efficient manner with limited regard for customer needs and preferences. A more balanced view involving both marketing and operations must prevail for long-run success.

CONCLUSION

The importance of marketing as a management function to both business and nonbusiness organizations lies in the fact that it links the organization to its environment. Success in raising funds from donors, in attracting volunteers, in selling services to individual or institutional customers, and in encouraging people to adopt new patterns of behavior requires, in each case, an understanding of the characteristics and current behavior patterns of those in the target group. Marketing research projects may be required to gain this knowledge, although sometimes existing information will provide the needed answers. A marketing strategy is composed of many elements that must be brought together in a coherent and consistent manner. Key issues in marketing strategy development include understanding the nature and size of the market, determining alternative ways of dividing the market into segments, and deciding which of these segments to serve. The strategy selected should reflect an assessment of the degree of competition (if any) within each market segment and the ability of the marketer to develop a successful product offering that both meets market needs and serves the institutional mission.

5

Business Planning for Nonprofit Enterprise

CYNTHIA W. MASSARSKY

THE MAIN TOOL FOR BUSINESS DEVELOPMENT is the business plan. A business plan is a formal, written plan that describes the business—what it does, how it does it, and why. It is the distillation of a massive amount of research into a comprehensive, coherent, and concise document. Emerging businesses need a written plan to force careful thinking, encourage discipline, forge internal communication, and enhance coordination and clarity of purpose among their managers and investors. They need a business plan to determine the amount of capital required, and to help raise it. And, once the business is operating, they need a yardstick against which to define and measure their progress.

HOW DOES NONPROFIT BUSINESS PLANNING DIFFER FROM FOR-PROFIT BUSINESS PLANNING?

In the broadest sense, nonprofit business planning does not differ greatly from for-profit business planning. Both examine the industry and the market for the venture's product or service, spell out operating and marketing plans, identify organization and management needs, and translate goals into monetary terms via pro forma financial statements (pro forma means "projected"). Both determine the purpose(s) for writing a business plan (e.g., to raise capital), and to couch the writing in terms of the audience they wish to address.

Differences surface, however, when analyzing the goals of each. In general, the primary goal of private sector enterprise is to make money for its owners. Enterprise among nonprofits, however, often exhibits several equally important goals. The goals may not always be consonant.

For example, a home for youth ex-offenders may have two goals: to earn a profit through the sale of a product, and to manufacture the product and sell it using the nonprofit's own clients. This dual agenda, mixing retail sales and manufacture with manpower training, will have an impact on every aspect of the business, from its legal structure and ability to raise capital, to its management team, operating procedures, marketing plan, and "bottom line." Multiple goals make business planning more complex and harder to perform.

Business plans of nonprofit organizations often reflect a social commitment. They incorporate the mission of their organizations into the plans. They seek to generate income, but not, for example, at the expense of the relationship between the nonprofit and the community in which it operates. This may mean that the nonprofit enterprise will operate on a break-even basis, or may generate only a minimal profit. If this is the case, capital for the business will not likely come from venture capitalists or financial institutions, which accept only low risk and expect a high return on their investments. Rather, funds will most likely come from government or foundation sources, which often accept high-risk ventures and expect a low (if any) return.

PERFORMING THE BUSINESS PLANNING FUNCTION

When Is the Business Plan Written and Who Writes It?

The business plan is the natural successor to the feasibility study, the document that examines the various ways the business can operate and investigates the conditions that would make it profitable. It may be written before start-up (to raise capital) or after start-up (to raise additional capital, for credibility purposes, or for managerial planning). In either case, it is undertaken when the writer has gathered all the information necessary to prove that the business will succeed.

Anyone with a thorough understanding of the business, familiarity with the construction of financial statements, and strong writing skills is capable of creating a business plan. In the private sector, it is usually the entrepreneur or a small team of originators/owners/managers who write the plan.

In the nonprofit sector, several possibilities exist. One is for the organization to select a staff member, perhaps the potential new business manager, and assign him or her the task of developing the plan. Another possibility is for several staff to jointly write the plan. The team might include the executive director, the financial director, the development officer, the special projects manager, and even board members. Another option (more risky) is to hire the business manager in advance of start-up, and to require that the first task be the preparation of the plan. Lastly, an independent consultant may perform the work. Clearly, there are drawbacks and benefits to each approach.

The three most important considerations in determining who writes the business plan are the requisite skills, the available time, and a clear understanding of the relationship and interplay between the business and the exempt mission of the organization.

The primary advantage of choosing existing staff members to write the plan is that in-house personnel usually have great respect for the nonprofit mission. They will ensure that the key aspects of it are built into the plan. In addition, by writing the plan, staff gain a thorough understanding of the development of the business and can be consulted as the business grows.

There are several disadvantages, however, in choosing from existing personnel. First, senior staff often lack the time necessary to devote to these projects, and end up putting them on the back burner. Preparing for a business start-up is a full-time job and can't be accomplished on an ad hoc basis. Second, existing staff may have some but not all of the business skills necessary to complete the task. Third, although they may have an understanding both of the exempt mission and business, staff often find it difficult to combine the two in a strongly written document. This tension represents one of the greatest obstacles to success.

Nonprofits can overcome some of these disadvantages by hiring an enterprise manager immediately after completing a feasibility study—assuming the results are strongly positive. In this way, the business secures both talent and continuity. And, because the manager is involved in the planning stage, she or he brings an important historical perspective to running the business. However, to find a person who can understand and work under multiple goals, and who will work for a business which is not yet operating, is difficult. Nonprofits may, in fact, need to offer various incentives to attract qualified managers.

Nonprofits may seek out independent consultants to perform various business-planning tasks. They can secure financial, personnel, operations, and general planning skills, while avoiding the complexities and financial burden involved in hiring additional permanent staff. They can seek consultants with backgrounds in business, line experience in working with nonprofits, and those who are well versed in planning business ventures for nonprofit organizations. The key matter, if a consultant is found, is for the nonprofit to supervise the consultant closely and to be clear from the outset what tasks this person will perform.

Constructing the Business Plan

There are numerous traditional business planning guides on the market, many of them quite good, which discuss beginning a business and writing a business plan. Most guides outline six main components of a business plan:

- Executive summary
- Description of the business
- Market analysis and market plan
- Discussion of management and personnel and production or service delivery
- Financial plan
- Supporting documents

A business plan should be written, whether the enterprise is a free-standing, for-profit venture or an in-house program division. Since the nonprofit enterprise is increasingly common, and since, if it is successful, it can turn around and become a for-profit venture, we have chosen to use the case of a start-up, nonprofit venture with both social and revenue-producing goals. This section of the chapter follows the format above and suggests ways to enhance the business plan for the nonprofit's venture. The case study is a fictional composite of business plans from several nonprofit organizations. It is for the South Side Children's Products Company.

The Executive Summary

The executive summary is found on the first page following the table of contents. It is a one-page summary of the key business points. Because its quality usually determines whether the reader will continue, the executive summary must be compelling, interesting, and convincing.

The executive summary contains a description of the business (its product or service, method of operations, location, management structure), financial information (sales and revenues figures, number of employees, break-even point), and a closing statement on the purpose of the business plan.

The executive summary of the nonprofit's business plan should include a statement explaining the purpose of the new business. It should convince the reader that funding the venture furthers the exempt mission of the nonprofit.

The executive summary answers such questions as:

- What is the product or service?
- Whom will you sell it to?
- How will you sell it (retail, wholesale, mail order, distributors)?
- Who is the management team?
- How many employees will the business have?
- Where is the business located?
- How will the business operate?
- How does the business relate to your nonprofit organization?
- What are the sales projections for the first three years?
- What is your profit estimate for the first three years?
- When will the business break even?
- How much money do you need, and why?
- How will the money be repaid?

South Side Children's Products: Executive Summary

The South Side Children's Center, a 40-year-old nonprofit arts education organization in San Francisco, plans to create South Side Children's Products, the area's first children's soft-product design and production company operated by minority women.

South Side Children's Products will design and produce blankets, pillows, stuffed toys, and other soft products for children, made of handscreened cotton fabric, using children's artwork as the basis for its fabric designs. It will sell its products whole-sale to the high-end children's furnishings market.

The soft-products business will be managed by a team of three women who have a total of twenty years' experience in the design, production, and sale of children's soft products. The business will identify, train, and employ minority women from the community. Apprentices will work for South Side Children's Products for one year, after which the business will place them in related positions in the industry.

South Side Children's Products will gross $213,000 at the end of its first year of op-eration and $640,000 after three years. By the end of 36 months, it will employ 19 people, have trained at least six apprentices, and have a payroll of $275,000.

As a program of the Center, South Side Children's Products will help to diversify the Center's funding base and its reliance on government funding, and will further its mission to enhance local economic development efforts by providing training and employment to minority women.

The sum of $130,000 is needed to purchase capital equipment and to cover operat-ing expenses until the business is profitable. South Side Children's Products requires two grants, $100,000 disbursable by month one and $30,000 disbursable by month four. South Side Children's Products does not anticipate any other need for grant support. Expansion and training will be financed from internal sources.

Description of the Business

This section describes the business venture in greater detail. It discusses the product or service, introduces market research results, and identifies unique characteristics that indicate success. The business description makes clear whether the venture is a start-up, expansion, or acquisition. It generally explains how the business will operate and relates the experience of its management team. It projects sales and net income for at least three years, determines break-even, and outlines any capital requirements.

For the nonprofit, the business section should also place the activity in the context of its exempt mission. It should identify why the business will be successful, point to the legal and operating relationship between the nonprofit and the new business, and stress how the business will capitalize on the expertise, talents, contacts, or goodwill of the organization.

The business section answers such questions as:

- What is the product or service?
- Who is the target market?
- Is the business a start-up, expansion, or acquisition?
- Is the business retail, wholesale, manufacturing, service?
- How will the business operate?
- Who is the management team?
- What are the projected sales and net income?
- What are the unique characteristics indicating success?

South Side Children's Products: The Business

South Side Children's Products will specialize in the design and production of soft products for children. It will sell its soft products exclusively to the wholesale children's furnishings market.

South Side Children's Products will operate as a program of the South Side Children's Center, a highly respected art-education organization for young people. It will further the mission of the Center by earning money to sustain current programs and nurture new ones while simultaneously providing training and employment for minority women in various aspects of the soft-product design and production trades.

Soft products encompass a range of merchandise from dolls and tote bags to quilts and pillows. South Side Children's Products line will target the high-end children's market, especially furnishings for babies' rooms, and will include quilts, crib and bed covers, wall hangings, covered hangers, mobiles, and stuffed toys. The business will also offer coordinated fabric by the yard.

South Side Children's Products will develop a line of ten different items and prepare "sewing kits" that include pre-cut patterns for use with the company's handscreened cotton fabric. Minority women from the community will assemble the kits for South Side Children's Products and be paid on an hourly basis.

Several key factors will give South Side Children's Products strong appeal and a competitive advantage in the marketplace. First, and most important, the business will be the only company which culls its fabric designs from the artwork of children. The designs will be a direct adaptation of the artwork of the children who participate in the Center's programs. The Center has written and verbal confirmation from designers, producers, and wholesale purchasers of children's soft products and fabric that there is significant demand for these designs (see Appendix A for letters of support).

Second, the business will draw upon the talents of the Center staff, who will adapt the children's designs, which lend themselves to reproduction on cotton fabric. In addition, staff are quite familiar with the handscreen process, and will assist in training apprentices.

Third, the business will be managed by a team of three women who have a total of 20 years' experience in the industry (see resumes, Appendix B). The technical and sales experience they have developed will be incorporated into South Side Children's Products. South Side Children's Products will be the only firm selling handscreened cotton fabric and soft products of such quality and unique design that is owned and operated by minority women.

Fourth, the Center has already identified several retailers who are interested in carrying the South Side Children's Products line. Since the visibility and availability of South Side Children's Products fabric and soft products will be key to its success, this interest indicates both the artistic attractiveness and commercial promise of the proposed business (see Appendix C for a list of these retailers).

Finally, the business will take advantage of the cost savings that will result from combining a design and handscreen fabric and soft products production in one location, as well as from capitalizing on the Center's staff expertise and shop facilities.

In the first year, the business will sell a total of 7,100 units with an average wholesale price of $30 per unit. It will market the various items wholesale to showrooms and retail shops that specialize in sophisticated furnishings for children. Sales are expected to be $213,000, with a gross margin of $143,322.

Market Analysis and Marketing Plan

The market analysis shows the reader that there is sufficient demand and willingness to pay for the product or service. Further, the data derived from the market analysis form the basis for the pro forma financial statements.

This section typically begins with a discussion of the "industry"—its size, trends over the last five to ten years, its current status (stable, growing, declining), and key factors that may positively or negatively affect sales (social, demographic, economic, technological).

Next, the analysis focuses on the specific market for the venture's product or service. It examines the size of the market and its growth potential, the characteristics of the typical consumer, and the competition.

The quality of the market analysis for the venture will not differ significantly from that of a for-profit business. The nonprofit must perform a statistically accurate analysis that is replicable and reliable.

Unlike major corporations, most nonprofits do not have a large amount of money to spend on market research. (To be sure, neither does small business.) Therefore, nonprofits must carefully choose the type of research and the researchers that will generate the best information for the dollars spent. For example, the nonprofit might use qualified volunteers or college students to conduct telephone surveys, or it might have a business-school class prepare and conduct a mass-mailing survey.

Of course, this surveying needs to be matched by searches of publicly available data in libraries, research institutions, chambers of commerce, industry associations, and various government agencies (such as the Bureau of Labor Statistics).

Although it is certainly true that "you get what you pay for," and that the quality of the information obtained is usually in direct proportion to the dollars spent, it is also important to consider the research phase in relation to the goal of the nonprofit business. If the goal is modest, perhaps to generate enough revenue to provide gainful employment to a handful of local residents, then the nonprofit may choose to conduct only a small amount of targeted quality research and hope that the results will point to achieving its goal.

Because products and services will not market themselves, the nonprofit should prepare a written marketing plan. The plan is a systematic way of organizing the analysis of the market, the organization's position in the market, and its program for future marketing activities. It describes how the business will attract and keep its customers, and its pricing policies in relation to the competition. It details: 1) the external environment (political, economic, technological, funders/backers, competition); 2) the internal environment (objectives, strengths, weaknesses); 3) problems and opportunities; 4) marketing goals and targets; 5) marketing strategies relating to target segments, competitive position, and the marketing mix; 6) a budget; 7) a marketing action plan; and 8) a monitoring system. This written plan will help nonprofits to choose wisely among options, coordinate activities of different parts of the organization, and anticipate and meet market challenges before they occur.

The market analysis and marketing plan answer such questions as:

- Who is the target market?
- Who is the typical consumer (age, sex, profession, income, buying habits)?
- What is the present size of the market?
- What percent of the market will the business have?
- How will the business expand its market?
- What is the market's growth potential?
- What geographical area will the business serve?
- Who is the competition? What are their strengths and weaknesses? How are they different from the business venture?
- What is the business' competitive edge?
- How will the business advertise and promote its product and service?
- How will the business distribute its product or provide its service?
- Are there any warranties or service policies?
- What is the business' pricing strategy?
- Will the business sell wholesale or retail? Will it have a sales force or use a marketing rep?
- Does seasonality affect the business?
- How will the business handle the public relations function?
- Will the business conduct ongoing research and development?

South Side Children's Products: The Market

South Side Children's Products will design and produce accessories for children's rooms. The soft-products market, as it is known today, is a quarter-of-a-billion-dollar industry, is about 12 years old, and is experiencing rapid growth. Continued growth is predicted.

Although the consumers of high-end home furnishings for children comprise only 5 percent of the population, they represent the greatest percentage of dollars spent. There are two types of purchasers of high-end home furnishings for children. The first is an executive (and his or her family), who is between 30–45 years old, earns upwards of $60,000 a year, has two or three children, and decorates children's rooms in a new home, apartment, or weekend/vacation retreat.

First-time parents over 30 years of age comprise a second relevant group. There is a strong high-end market emerging that takes advantage of the age, sophistication, and economic capacity of this population group, its family, and friends. One design firm in Chicago caters exclusively to this group of clients. Its customers spend an average of $5,000 to decorate a nursery or child's room, which includes the purchase of soft products as well as coordinating fabric. South Side Children's Products is well positioned for this growth market.

Direct sources of competition for South Side Children's Products are the many firms that create designs for handscreen printing, as well as several production companies that purchase designs and handscreen them on yardage for the wholesale home furnishings market. Many are established, well respected businesses that produce a high-quality product.

In addition, approximately 20 companies produce soft-product items made from fabric, of which four hold the greatest market share. Some of the competition, including Marimekko, target other markets as well as the children's furnishings market. They use the same fabric designs to make "standard" soft goods for the kitchen, bed, bath, and living rooms. There is no indication whatsoever that this market is either saturated or difficult to enter. In fact, there is strong indication that small companies are succeeding in this business in a big way.

South Side Children's Products will cut into the national market in four ways: by specifically targeting the growing high-end children's furnishings market; by producing products that are distinguished for their uniquely creative, yet useful designs; by using fabric designs that have a strong appeal because they are based on the artwork of children, which is in fact the actual target market; and by ensuring that the fabric and items remain special by restricting their sale to exclusive shops catering to the high-end baby furnishings market (see Appendix D for a list of possible items for manufacture).

Unlike the competition, South Side Children's Products will capitalize on its own story—that of a San Francisco-based nonprofit organization that has created an income-earning arm to employ local residents to produce unique designs and products for sale—and to use the income generated to support programs. The business of South Side Children's Products will be highly attractive to the trade and media because of its creative ingenuity and its training and economic development components. The press it receives will inspire consumers to seek out the South Side Children's Products collection.

South Side Children's Products will sell its product line through selected advertising and personal selling, and by conducting a well targeted public relations campaign. In addition, South Side Children's Products will regularly exhibit at gift and toy shows. The business will contract with reps where appropriate (see Appendix E for a detailed marketing plan).

Management, Personnel, and Organizational Structure

The management section is probably most crucial to the business plan and to its readers. Because it is generally known that a high percentage of business failure is attributed to managerial weakness, the business plan must present a strong management team, and, in its absence, the ability and contacts to obtain key staff.

This section of the business plan discusses executive management. It tells how their background and experience relates to the business venture and how it will make the venture a success. It describes duties, responsibilities, reporting procedures, and decision-making authority. It may discuss their salaries and benefits.

The personnel section of the business plan discusses the current and projected personnel needs of the operation. It does this by describing the number of staff, full-time versus part-time work schedules, the training required, wages, overtime and benefits, and the supply of available workers.

The executive management and personnel discussion will include the relationship between the business staff and the staff of the nonprofit itself. Since several possibilities exist, the choice of organizational structure will also have to be discussed.

One possibility is for the venture (either nonprofit or for-profit) and the nonprofit organization to share management and/or personnel. When this is the case, the business plan must make clear the relationship between the two. For example, it must state which staff will be shared, what percentage of time will be devoted to each, and how staff will be compensated.

When management and personnel are shared, conflict sometimes arises in determining who will work for the business venture (business vs. nonprofit experience), in setting salary levels (business usually has to pay better than nonprofits), and in staff allegiance to one program over another. The nonprofit business that chooses to make use of shared personnel must present a convincing scenario in its business plan. Those that do not intend to share management or personnel must still contend with the perceived and real differences in requisite expertise and compensation (because business expertise may be required, higher levels of compensation may be necessary, and this may result in problems among staff).

A second possibility is for the new venture to train and employ the clients of the nonprofit organization. Here, conflicts often arise with respect to salaries, productivity, hours available for work, experience and skills, training, permanence, and consumer acceptance. In many instances there is a trade-off between profitability and the number of clients employed. But this need not be a hindrance so long as the nonprofit business plan reiterates its "dual agenda" and describes how the business anticipates and plans to deal with these issues.

This section answers such questions as:

Management

What is the business background of key management?
What is their managerial and operational experience (staff, line)?
What is their educational background?
Why will they make the business a success?
What are the responsibilities of each?
Who performs the planning function?
Who reports to whom?
Where are the final decisions made?
Is there a board of directors or advisory committee?
What is the overall organizational structure?
What outside professional services are required, and who will provide them?
How will management be compensated?

Personnel

How many staff will the business require in year 1, year 2, year 3?
What functions will each perform?
What skills must each have?
Are the positions full- or part-time?
Is training required?

How will personnel be compensated (hourly, wages, salaried, overtime, benefits)? Is there sufficient supply of skilled staff available in the marketplace?

South Side Children's Products: Management and Personnel

South Side Children's Products will be a program of the South Side Children's Center, but will have its own staff. It will have an advisory board, which will include several SSCC board members, as well as new appointees with relevant business experience. Preliminary research indicates that there is strong demand for both apprentice and kit-assembler positions. Figure 1 depicts the South Side Children's Products structure. (Appendix B presents the resumes of key management.)

South Side Children's Products: Job Descriptions

Business manager: The president and business manager of South Side Children's Products will be the current assistant director of SSCC, Barbara Jones. Ms. Jones helped to found SSCC in 1969. Since then SSCC has grown to a staff of fifteen with a budget of $575,000. Ms. Jones will leave her position as assistant director of SSCC, will have overall policy control for South Side Children's Products, and will be responsible for all aspects of its undertaking, to the executive director of SSCC.

The business manager directs the daily operations of South Side Children's Products and supervises the production manager and marketing and sales manager. Along with the production and marketing and sales managers, she determines how a work order will be produced, how it fits into the daily schedule, and which staff performs each task. The business manager helps the apprentices and other workers with problems that may arise on the job, oversees machine operations and maintenance, and orders supplies.

The business manager's position also involves order fulfillment, general personnel management, and administration of all daily business activities, including invoicing, paying bills, record keeping, developing written policies and pricing strategies, and preparing periodic status reports. The business manager is responsible for all vendor and customer relations.

Starting salary for the president and business manager is $30,000. Ms. Jones' resume is found in Appendix B.

Production manager: The production manager is Janet Burns. She has two main responsibilities. One is to create designs for handscreen printing and run the production of yardage. This involves reviewing the children's artwork and adapting or editing the ones most appropriate for fabric design. She works the repeat (layout) and explores various colorings and colorways or color combinations. She oversees the photocopying process, table registration, color separation, and screenmaking. She also creates or supervises the creation of the designs, patterns, and samples for the soft products. The production manager is responsible for supervising the trainees and apprentices in these tasks.

The second responsibility of the production manager is to coordinate the production and distribution of the soft products. She ensures that the fabric is printed, and that the kits are prepared and that the soft products are constructed. She recruits, trains, and supervises the kit assemblers.

Starting salary for the production manager is $25,000. Ms. Burns' resume is found in Appendix B.

FIGURE 1. SOUTH SIDE CHILDREN'S PRODUCTS
ORGANIZATION CHART

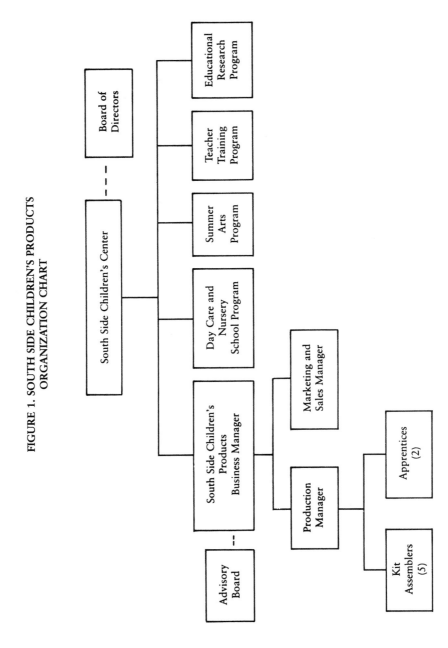

Marketing and sales manager: The marketing and sales manager is Susan French. Her job involves marketing/promotion/sales, with coordinated responsibilities in setting pricing policy, preparing quotes for custom orders, and maintaining records on sales and volume. The marketing specialist's job is to spread the South Side Children's Products name, and to show and sell its product lines. She develops an annual marketing strategy which involves planning the "opening"; identifying representatives within the San Francisco metropolitan area, as well as other cities; personal selling and booking space at the trade shows; preparing and executing promotional campaigns; and conducting market research where appropriate.

Starting salary for the marketing and sales manager is $25,000. Ms. French's résumé is found in Appendix B.

Trainees/apprentices: The training program teaches trainees all aspects of the screen-print process, enabling them to gain further employment in this specialty area. Two trainees each year will become apprentices—regular employees of the company. Trainees and apprentices report to the production manager, and are responsible for producing yardage and the soft-product sewing kits. They also learn about small business and financial management and sales and promotion. No prior experience in design or screen printing is necessary, but trainees must demonstrate a strong interest in learning the trade. Apprentices are hired for four hours' work per day at $3.50 per hour.

Kit assemblers: Kit assemblers produce or manufacture soft goods using the kits supplied by the fabric production staff. Each assembler receives a pattern(s), the necessary supplies, and instruction on how to sew each item. Equipment is supplied by the business. Kit assemblers are required to produce a product of high quality and according to time schedule. They are full-time employees of the business who receive compensation on an hourly basis, at $5.00 per hour.

Production/Service Delivery

This section describes the specific operational policies and plans for production or service delivery. The main goal of the production/service delivery section is to demonstrate that management understands and has prepared for all the steps that are necessary to produce its product or service.

Because enterprise among nonprofits is still somewhat unfamiliar to many, the production/service delivery section for the nonprofit's business plan should include evidence that indicates some expertise and experience in this area. This does not mean that it is necessary for the organization to have been in business, but rather that it has a track record in processes that are the same or similar to those of the new venture. For example, a social service agency may have ten years of experience in providing counseling services to drug and alcohol abusers, although it never charged a fee for its service. This agency would probably have a good understanding of the marketplace, its clients, and the mechanics of providing counseling services, which translate into marketing, service delivery information, and plans.

The demonstration project is also common among nonprofit organizations, and this too may be used as evidence of operational experience. For example, a sheltered workshop that intends to employ its own clients to produce a product for sale in the marketplace might refer to its success in training the disabled to work in an assembly-line fashion.

The business operations sections answers such questions as:

- What is the process required to manufacture the item for sale, or to provide the service?
- Which aspects of this process will the business undertake, and which will be provided by others? Who will provide them?
- What are the requirements for fixtures, furniture, machinery or other equipment?
- Will seasonality affect production/service delivery?
- What is the floor plan and structural features of the facility?
- How will the business design new products or develop new services?
- How will the business purchase inventory/supplies?
- How will the business administer quality and cost controls?
- How will the business benefit from the experience of the nonprofit organization?

South Side Children's Products: Production

Last year, the South Side Children's Center operated a training program, which simultaneously taught young women the design and handscreen print fabric process and provided a demonstration model for South Side Children's Products. It was run by Janet Burns, an established designer/printer, who, along with other staff, purchased supplies, prepared the physical space, and worked with the students.

The experience proved four important concepts: 1) there is interest and talent among women in the South Side to learn the design and print trade, 2) there is a wealth of designs available through the Center, which are particularly adaptable to the children's furnishings market, 3) it is both possible and desirable to combine aspects of training and production in the handscreen fabric business, and 4) the methods employed to train women to design and print fabric can be applied to the design and production of soft products.

With this positive experience as a base, Barbara Jones and Janet Burns began to investigate the possibility of turning the project into an ongoing business. Last fall, they selected designs and prototype products to compose the first collection. South Side Children's Products can now begin its first month of production.

There are several processes required to produce fabric and soft products for the children's furnishings market. First, to produce the fabric, the production manager adapts the designs chosen to be in the collection, works the repeat, prepares the screens, and chooses the colorings. She then prepares the tables for printing and works with trainees in printing the fabric. When the fabric has dried, it is sent out to be cured.

Next, the cured fabric is cut according to pattern, and is put into sewing kits along with other items necessary to produce the soft products. The kits are inventoried on shelves.

The kit assemblers or sewers sew the soft goods, according to the schedule set by the business manager and production manager. This schedule reflects current and anticipated orders by type of product and fulfillment date. Finished products are either boxed and shipped immediately, or are inventoried on shelves.

The production manager ensures that the appropriate paperwork is completed and given to the business manager for bookkeeping purposes. In addition, the production manager keeps the business manager informed of the need for supplies. These are purchased from vendors once the appropriate bids have been collected.

A list of capital equipment requirements appears in Appendix F. A floor plan appears in Appendix G.

Financial Plan

The financial plan is the section of the business plan that pulls the sales projections and cost estimates together. The financial plan outlines the following: 1) the business' income, assets required to generate income, and the sources and amounts of funds that are required to finance the assets; and 2) solvency, i.e., the business' ability to cover cash outflows with cash inflows over time. The financial plan is only as sound as the assumptions and the data on which it is based. It is crucial that business projections be comprehensive and accurate. Most financial planners suggest that the authors of plans use conservative financial projections, which underestimate revenue and overestimate expenses. Sound financial projections and well-executed statements are necessary, whether the new venture is capitalized by debt, equity, grants, or some combination of sources, and whether capitalized by a bank, foundation, board of trustees, or other interested party. The same basic information is required for any business plan, regardless of sector. (See the chapter by Ellen Arrick for further discussion of financing issues.)

The form of the financial statements may differ, however, depending on the legal status of the nonprofit's business, i.e., whether it is a for-profit subsidiary or an income-generating program of the nonprofit. The statements may follow private sector accounting principles, fund accounting principles, or a combination of the two. The important point to remember is that the financial plan should take a form that best reflects the nature of the business and its relationship to the nonprofit organization.

Many private sector financial planners would advise a new venture group to hire an accountant to develop the necessary pro forma statements if no one on the team has the knowledge and expertise to do so. Still, the nonprofit organization embarking on a new venture will benefit significantly from the hands-on experience of preparing its own statements.

First, in preparing the statements, the business' planners are forced to understand every aspect of the business and to feel certain that its operations are designed to achieve maximum efficiency. Second, in projecting revenue and expense figures, planners are forced to check all their assumptions and verify all estimates. Third, by playing an active role, the planners are in the best position to explain the business plan and its financial projections when seeking funding. Finally, by immersing themselves in the venture from the start, the business' planners will run a better operation.

The financial plan for a new venture includes three types of pro forma documents. These documents should be prepared for the venture, regardless of whether it is a program of the nonprofit or a wholly owned for-profit subsidiary:

TABLE I. SOUTH SIDE CHILDREN'S PRODUCTS: PRO FORMA CASH-FLOW PROJECTIONS 19X1

							Month						
	1	2	3	4	5	6	7	8	9	10	11	12	Total
Cash receipts													
Sales	—	—	10,080	14,400	14,400	17,280	21,600	21,600	24,480	28,800	28,800	31,680	213,120
Grants	100,000	—	—	30,000	—	—	—	—	—	—	—	—	130,000
Total receipts	100,000	—	—	44,400	14,400	17,280	21,600	21,600	24,480	28,800	28,800	31,680	343,120
Cash disbursements													
Cost of goods sold	—	840	1,200	1,200	1,440	1,800	1,800	2,040	2,400	2,400	2,640	3,000	20,760
Variable labor and taxes	—	2,448	3,218	3,218	3,732	4,502	4,502	4,016	5,016	5,016	6,300	7,070	49,038
Salaries and taxes	7,133	8,441	8,441	8,441	8,441	8,441	8,441	8,441	8,441	8,441	8,441	8,441	99,984
Disability	—	—	697	—	—	697	—	—	697	—	—	697	2,788
Rent	—	—	—	—	—	—	—	—	—	—	—	—	—
Utilities	—	—	—	—	—	—	—	—	—	—	—	—	—
Maintenance	—	—	—	—	—	—	—	—	—	—	—	—	—
Telephone	300	300	300	300	300	300	300	300	300	300	300	300	3,600
Office supplies	50	50	50	50	50	50	50	50	50	50	50	50	600
Marketing	8,000	5,000	—	—	—	—	5,000	—	—	—	—	—	18,000
Insurance	1,000	—	—	1,000	—	—	1,000	—	—	1,000	—	—	4,000
Legal	625	—	—	625	—	—	625	—	—	625	—	—	2,500
Accounting	625	—	—	625	—	—	625	—	—	625	—	—	2,500
Travel	250	250	250	250	250	250	250	250	250	250	250	250	3,000
Capital expense	28,130	—	—	—	—	—	—	—	—	—	—	—	28,130
Miscellaneous	1,000	1,000	1,000	1,000	1,000	1,000	1,000	1,000	1,000	1,000	1,000	1,000	12,000
Total disbursements	47,113	18,329	15,156	16,709	15,213	17,040	23,593	16,097	18,154	19,707	18,981	20,808	246,900
Net cash flow	52,887	(18,329)	(5,076)	27,691	(813)	240	(1,993)	5,503	6,326	9,093	9,819	10,872	96,220
Cumulative cash flow	52,887	34,558	29,482	57,173	56,360	56,600	54,607	60,110	66,436	75,529	85,348	96,220	

TABLE II. SOUTH SIDE CHILDREN'S PRODUCTS: PRO FORMA INCOME STATEMENT
12/31/x1

Support and revenue:	
Grants	$130,000
Net sales	213,120
Less: cost of goods sold	69,798
Gross margin	$143,322
Total support and revenue	$273,322
Operating expense:	
Salaries and taxes	99,984
Disability	2,788
Telephone	3,600
Office supplies	600
Marketing	18,000
Travel	3,000
Insurance	4,000
Legal	2,500
Accounting	2,500
Depreciation	2,813
Miscellaneous	12,000
Total operating expenses	$151,785
Net profit (loss)	$121,537

- Pro forma income statements
- Pro forma cash flows
- Pro forma balance sheets

The cash flow statement should be projected monthly, and the income statements and balance sheets annually for the first three years. In addition, the statements should be accompanied by notes that explain and document the assumptions on which they are based.

A financial plan for a new business also typically includes a statement of financial requirements. This statement sets forth the amount, type, and source of funds required for business start-up, capital equipment, and working capital. It is easily derived from the three primary statements mentioned above.

A cash flow statement, income statement, balance sheet, statement of financial requirements, and notes to the financial projections for South Side Children's Products appear in Tables I-V.

Cash Flow Statement

The cash flow statement attempts to budget the cash needs of the business, and shows *cash in* and *cash out* on a monthly basis. It shows how much cash will be needed, when

TABLE III. SOUTH SIDE CHILDREN'S PRODUCTS:
PRO FORMA BALANCE SHEET
12/31/x1

Assets	
Current Assets:	
Cash	$ 86,150
Receivables	—
Inventory, at cost	10,070
Total current assets	96,220
Fixed assets:	
Furniture, equipment and leasehold improvements	28,130
Less: accumulated depreciation	2,813
Net building and equipment	25,317
Total assets	$121,537
Liabilities and fund balances	
Current liabilities:	
Accounts payable	—
Notes payable	—
Total current liabilities	—
Fund balances:	
Current funds	96,220
Investment in furniture, equipment and leasehold improvements	25,317
Total liabilities and fund balances	$121,537

it will be needed, and where it will come from. This projection is probably the most central item to the business plan because it shows whether or not there is sufficient cash on hand to run the business.

Every bit of information gleaned from the research is used in the cash flow projection. The statement is constructed in several steps. First, the appropriate revenue and expense amounts are filled in by month. Then, for each month, expenses are subtracted from revenues to arrive at a net cash flow. Finally, the net cash flow for month one is added to the net cash flow for month two to arrive at the cumulative cash flow for month two, and so on across the statement. In essence, it is like accounting for

TABLE IV. SOUTH SIDE CHILDREN'S PRODUCTS: STATEMENT OF FINANCIAL
REQUIREMENTS

Item	Funds Required	Date Required	Source
Capital Equipment	$ 28,130	Month1	Grant
Working Capital	71,870	Month1	Grant
Working Capital	30,000	Month4	Grant
Total	$130,000		

TABLE V. NOTES TO THE FINANCIAL PROJECTIONS 19X1

Income
  Sales are based on an average unit wholesale price of $30.
  On average, customers order 4 items at 1 dozen each.
  Customers reorder the same quantity 3 times per year, or every 4 months.
  Customers' terms are cash or net 10.

Expense
  Costs of goods sold, excluding variable labor, are $2.50 per unit.
  Variable labor and taxes include total wages for apprentice printers and wages for sewers
    to complete units required for the subsequent month, at the following rates:

    2 apprentice printers each @ $3.50/hour, 20 hours/week
    5 sewers each @ $5.00/hour, 40 hours/week

  Apprentice printers print and cut the yardage. It takes a sewer one hour to complete a
    unit.
  Salaries and taxes include wages paid to sewers to build inventory, and annual salaries for
    administration, as follows:

Business manager	$30,000
Director of marketing and sales	$25,000
Production manager	$25,000

  South Side Children's Products does not offer personnel benefits.
  The parent, South Side Children's Center, provides space, utilities, and custodial
    maintenance at no cost to South Side Children's Products.

deposits made and checks written in a checking account and calculating a cash balance.
    Although performing these calculations is easy, determining what numbers to utilize
is not. For example, *cash receipts* refer to all cash coming in, including:

- Cash at the beginning of the period
- Cash from the sales of products/services made and received during the month
- Cash from the sales of products/services made during prior months but received in
  this month
- Cash received from grants, loans
- Cash received from assets sold
- Cash received from equity investment
- Cash received from recovery of bad debts

    In projecting sales, for example, it is necessary to apply the research to estimate the
total dollar amount of annual sales. If the business is selling fabric, planners must
determine the number of yards of each design that will be sold and the price of each
yard for each design. Then, of that total annual amount, they must project how much
will be sold during each month of the year. They need to know about seasonality, for
example, if particular times during the year are better or worse for the sale of the
product or service.

The statement will also reflect a sales policy—that is, if prepayment is required, if payment is required within 30 days of the sale, if a partial prepayment is due, if payment is C.O.D., etc. This determines the month in which cash is received.

Although grants and loans may be listed as one of the first items on the cash flow, this item is typically dealt with last. In other words, the entire cash flow was constructed without filling in anything under the grants or loans columns. Then, business planners look at the position at the end of each month (net and cumulative cash flow lines) to see if there is enough income to cover expenses. If, for example, there are negative cumulations, the high point will determine the minimum amount of working capital needed to cover capital expenses.

When the amount of money needed is determined, it is plugged in prior to the month when it is needed, and the entire cash flow is recalculated. (Computer programs such as Lotus 1-2-3 do this recalculation automatically.) The cash may be in the form of a grant, a loan, the sale of equity, etc. If it is a loan, the statement must reflect a debt service payment under the expense or disbursement part of the cash flow.

Cash disbursements refer to all cash going out, for example:

- New inventory purchased
- Salaries, wages, benefits, taxes
- Rent, utilities
- Fees: accounting, legal, consulting
- Insurance
- Debt service
- New/used equipment purchased
- Transportation, freight
- Advertising
- Provision for past due accounts/bad debts
- Contingency
- Dividends, taxes (for a for-profit organization)

To a certain degree, many expense projections relate directly to sales projections. In the case study of South Side Children's Products, monthly wages are tied to the monthly amount of units sold. And this relates back to the market research. Furthermore, the managers need to know how much it will cost in inventory, utilities, freight, etc., to make one unit, as well as the number of employees needed to do so. They also need to know how much to spend for advertising and promotion each month to meet monthly sales projections.

Cash or payment is not always received in the month that the sale is made, and sometimes it is not received at all. (This would be an allowance for bad debt or uncollectibles.) On the other hand, expenses such as salaries are incurred in the month that the sale is made. Business planners must constantly remember that they are constructing a monthly cash in/cash out statement and not an annual revenue and expense budget.

Another point to remember is that some monthly expenses may be fixed expenses— that is, expenses that are the same each month because they are not dependent on the number of units produced or gross sales. South Side Children's Products shows fixed cash disbursements, such as certain salaries, or insurance, legal, and accounting fees.

And finally, although certain items such as depreciation are expenses, they do not appear in the cash flow because they do not represent an actual outlay of cash. (Depreciation is the process of recognizing the cost of an asset [furniture, equipment] as an expense during each year of its estimated service life.)

The cash flow projection serves several purposes. For one thing, it is an essential component of the business plan, and it shows an investor, lender, or interested party where the business expects to be, on a cash basis, at various points in time.

It also shows the business' planners the same thing. For purposes of the new venture (and the business plan), planners will want to carefully examine the monthly net cash flow, to get their revenue and expenses under control.

Business planners should look carefully at the monthly cumulative cash flow. Are there enough months where revenue exceeds expense to cover those when it does not? It may be acceptable to show one or more negative net cash flow figures as long as the cumulative cash flow figures are positive.

If there is a negative cumulative cash flow figure, this is a warning sign. It means that, according to best projections, there will not be enough cash to cover expenses. Planners will have to go back and reevaluate revenue and expenses, and adjust them. For example, they may inject more capital through a loan or a grant (or equity participation if a for-profit). Or, they may want to adjust sales or expense figures. This recalibration cannot be done willy-nilly. Adjustments should be based on realistic, conservative, market-based estimates, and when an adjustment is made in one area, such as sales, it usually means making an adjustment in several other areas, such as variable labor, inventory, advertising, etc.

Cash flow projections should also be used as a budget to course-correct when the operation gets underway. If expenses for a given item increase over the amount allotted for a given month, the business' managers should find out why and take corrective action. And corrective action includes adjusting the entire statement to reflect the new information.

If expenses are less than expected, the business should also find out why. Original projections may have been overestimated, managers may have found a better way to economize, or they may have neglected to pay a bill!

Income Statement

The pro forma income statement measures how successfully management will be able to use the business' resources to predict how profitable the business will be. Also called the profit-and-loss statement (P and L), the income statement projects the difference between net income (sales minus the cost of sales) and operating expenses for a given period of time. Cost of sales are the costs directly attributed to producing the product or service that is sold. For example, they can include such items as raw materials, direct labor, and possibly equipment in a manufacturing business.

In generating pro forma income statements, projections for the second and third year are usually logical extensions of first-year figures. However, it is important to realize that, depending on the business, not all revenue and expense projections will increase by the same proportion each month or year. One type of business may have large start-up expenditures. Another may have a long lead time before making its first sale. Other businesses are seasonal, with the bulk of sales occurring in one part of the year and the bulk of expenses during another.

In still other ways, the bottom line on the income statement over several years is directly related to the type of business venture. Expenses do not always grow at the same rate as sales. For example, in manufacturing some expenses remain relatively fixed over time, such as office and professional services, while others increase with sales, such as payroll and shipping. Looking at the differences between fixed and variable costs in relation to sales helps to illuminate the true sources of expense.

Balance Sheet

The pro forma balance sheet summarizes the resources invested in the business by showing the business' assets, liabilities, and owners' equity at a given point in time. The balance sheet is divided into two sections. The first half lists *assets*—for example, cash, machinery and equipment, and inventory and supplies. The second half lists *liabilities* and *owners' equity*. Liabilities include items such as money due to vendors (accounts payable) and principal and interest due on a loan (debt). Current liabilities are owed to creditors during the first year of operation. Long-term liabilities are those owed for subsequent years. Owners' equity includes investments in the business by partners, stockholders, and others, as well as any retained earnings. In a balance sheet, assets must equal liabilities and owners' equity.

The balance sheet for the nonprofit's business (which either secures its own nonprofit status, or which remains a program of the nonprofit "parent") will show a *fund balance* instead of owners' equity. This is because by law nonprofit organizations cannot sell equity in their operations. In fact, they are "owned" by the states in which they reside. A fund balance, therefore, is merely equal to the difference between the business' assets and liabilities.

Supporting Documents

This section of the business plan is actually an appendix. It serves to expand on certain aspects of the business venture by supplying the reader with supplementary information that is less appropriate to the body of the plan. For the nonprofit's business plan, this provides an opportunity to include relevant and supportive materials relating to the nonprofit parent.

The supporting documents section, or appendix, generally includes such items as:

• Resumes of key management

- Market data—statistics
- List of product/service offerings
- Floor plan indicating requirements for space
- Capital-equipment list
- Quotes and estimates from vendors
- Rent, lease, or purchase agreements
- Letters indicating a line of credit or loan
- Letters of intent from potential customers
- Letters of support from others in the industry, or from foundations and corporate giving offices
- Legal documents, such as incorporation papers or nonprofit status determination letter
- Annual report and financial statement of the nonprofit parent

South Side Children's Products: Supporting Documents

Appendix A: Letters of support from designers, producers, and wholesalers
Appendix B: Resumes of key management
Appendix C: List of retailers interested in carrying South Side Children's Products
Appendix D: List of possible items for manufacture
Appendix E: Marketing plan
Appendix F: List of capital equipment requirements
Appendix G: Floor plan of South Side Children's Products

CONCLUSION

Although they are faced with an arduous task, nonprofit organizations wishing to venture into the business arena should not be put off by the rigorous thinking, research, and financial planning involved in preparing business plans. It is through these activities that business planners and nonprofit managers will take meaningful and productive steps towards reaching the social and economic goals of the organizations they serve.

6

Financing the Enterprise

ELLEN ARRICK

THE NONPROFIT ENTREPRENEUR, like the for-profit entrepreneur, has to wear two hats in going about the business of locating financing for an enterprise. He or she has to be promotional, i.e., perform the function of a cheerleader rallying resources in order to make the project happen. But, more importantly, he or she also has to be coldly analytical about what it takes to make the project financially viable. The financing strategy that gives the project the best chance of success has to be determined; that strategy also has to be adjusted in the event that things do not work out as planned.

Lenders and investors are first of all interested in the project's viability. If their assessment is that the project will not succeed financially, promotion of its program-matic merits will not help to convince them. Lenders and investors tend to think in terms of *risk* and *return*: "How much risk is there that I will lose my investment? Is the return that I'm likely to receive sufficient to offset this risk?"

This chapter is aimed at helping the nonprofit entrepreneur to see his or her enterprise the way that lenders and investors do. The focus here is on helping the nonprofit entrepreneur to evaluate the financial risks associated with the enterprise, and to identify and implement a financing strategy appropriate to those risks. The first step in this process is to ask a series of questions about characteristics of the enterprise, and assign a risk factor (high, medium, or low) to the project, based on the answers to those questions. Then, by looking at the risks associated with all of the characteristics of the enterprise taken as a whole, the entrepreneur can develop a financing plan that matches the overall risk of the project. The initial phase of this process can be called *building a risk profile*. Lenders and investors perform this step automatically—almost intuitively. They will quickly scan a business plan and pick out the key characteristics, mentally assign risk factors to them, and make a determination about whether to lend or invest. Nonprofit entrepreneurs need to go through this process, too. They need to analyze risk carefully, in order to anticipate the financial concerns of lenders, investors, and grantmakers.

BUILDING A RISK PROFILE

This section will set out the three basic questions that the entrepreneur needs to ask about the enterprise, and identify the kind of risk factors applied by lenders or investors to the various characteristics of the venture.

What kind of enterprise is it?

There are three types of enterprise that nonprofits pursue: 1) *real estate*, 2) *manufacturing*, and 3) *service* businesses. Each carries with it a different level of risk.

Real estate. This includes housing, commercial, and industrial development. It is perceived as the least risky type of venture for nonprofits, since it is much easier to define a market for real estate than it is to define it for a manufactured product or a service. Moreover, real estate ventures almost always offer collateral with a relatively easily identified value, one which tends to appreciate with time. Further, revenues (rentals or sales) and expenses (operations, debt service, maintenance, etc.) can be projected with a much greater degree of certainty than can those of the other types of ventures. Of the three types of real estate ventures, housing is considered least risky because there is such a scarcity of affordable housing that, if it can be priced in line with comparable housing in its location, the market for it is virtually guaranteed. In housing, the chief difficulty lies in assembling the financial package that makes it affordable, not in marketing the product.

Commercial and industrial real estate development is considered riskier than housing because the market demand for this space is much more difficult to gauge. Locating and evaluating tenants can be difficult, and revenues are subject to more uncertainty than housing. Industrial real estate development frequently involves making special modifications for tenants. If the space is vacated by one tenant, it may be hard to re-rent it.

Manufacturing. Producing a tangible product is riskier than developing real estate because it is much more difficult to predict revenues and expenses. In addition, manufacturing involves ongoing engineering, design, and production activities (unlike real estate, in which those are essentially one-time events). Manufacturing involves day-to-day marketing and labor management, unlike real estate development, in which marketing and labor are a much smaller component of operations. And, while equipment and inventory can frequently be used as collateral, they are more difficult to appraise, and they tend to lose, rather than gain, value.

Service businesses. These businesses represent the greatest risk to the lender or investor because there is rarely much in the way of collateral (equipment or inventory).

Moreover, service businesses generally have lower margins of profit than do manufacturing or real estate development. However, service businesses are usually easier for nonprofits to enter than manufacturing because they have much lower capital costs, and because they frequently parallel an existing activity of the nonprofit.

What kind of track record do the enterprise and its management have?

Another important factor in the risk profile is the amount of experience of the venture and/or its management. Because there are so many unknowns, start-ups are very difficult to finance, and start-ups with inexperienced management are the most difficult. A manufacturing or service business with no track record will be harder to finance than one already underway. Lenders and investors are most persuaded by successful, ongoing activity, which they believe to be the best indicator of the future success of the venture.

The risk of a start-up may be mitigated by establishing a *joint venture* with an experienced partner, who brings marketing and management skills or contacts to the arrangement in return for a share of the profits. For example, a nonprofit whose objective is employment generation might co-venture with a city contractor for bus shelters, with the nonprofit bringing in low-cost social investment dollars in return for guaranteed job slots. In this case, the experience that the for-profit partner brings in construction offsets the inexperience of the nonprofit partner.

Expansion. This is the least risky situation for which financing is sought. The venture has a track record against which future projections can be evaluated. However unreliable past experience is as a predictor of the future, lenders and investors take comfort in what is known. Needless to say, if the track record of the venture is poor, that will not help to reassure lenders and investors, unless clear reasons (unrelated to the quality of management or market demand) can be isolated and shown to be resolvable in the context of the expansion. For example, the margins of a venture might improve with an increase in volume that is only made possible by expansion.

What kind of financing is needed?

Finding the right answer to this question is vital to the success of the venture. The kind of financing that is *needed* may be different than the kind of financing that is *available*. It is important to identify what type of financing is appropriate for the expected revenue stream of the enterprise based on the timing and source of the revenues. For example, many nonprofit entrepreneurs confuse the need for cash flow financing with the need for working capital. Although the terms are frequently used interchangeably, the source and timing of repayment for cash flow and working capital financing are very different, as will be seen below. Because of this, lenders and investors assign very different levels of risk to requests for cash flow loans and working capital loans.

From a lender or investor's point of view, the key factors that go into the assessment of risk for a particular type of financing are: purpose of the loan, availability of collateral, predictability of the source of repayment, and amount of time it takes to recover the loan or investment. In general, the more uncertain the source of repayment, and the longer the period of recovery of investment, the more perceived risk there is to the funder. While many lenders will always insist on collateral, liquidation of collateral is always viewed as the last-resort source of repayment. This is because gaining possession may be difficult, time consuming, and costly. As a result, many loan requests which appear to be adequately collateralized are turned down because they do not offer a sufficiently predictable and timely source of repayment. It is crucial for the nonprofit entrepreneur to recognize and acknowledge the differences in risk associated with different types of financing needs, so that the appropriate source of capital is approached, and the appropriate type of financing is obtained.

Different types of financing needs imply different levels of risk, both to the venture and to the funder. Entrepreneurs need to recognize that risk works two ways. There is a risk to the lender or investor that the financing will not be repaid, or that return on the investor's capital will be insufficient. But taking on financing also implies some risk to the health of the venture itself. The wrong kind of financing will probably hurt, and possibly cause the failure of, the enterprise. Before borrowing money or accepting equity investment, management of a nonprofit enterprise needs to consider what the implications of financing are, both in terms of its effect on ongoing operations and in the event of failure to repay. Some of the possible implications include: control exercised by lender or investor over day-to-day operations, management changes, sale of assets, mergers or acquisitions, and potential to lose assets assigned to the lender in the event of a foreclosure.

The following section lists the most frequent types of financial needs that an enterprise might experience. They are ranked in *ascending* order of risk to lender or investor.

Cash Flow Financing

This type of need reflects a *timing* problem in the receipt of funds. It is utilized when the borrower needs cash to cover expenses in anticipation of revenues, when the revenues are related to a grant or contract. In this case, the loan *take out* or repayment is identifiable, i.e., comes from a source that can be predicted with a high degree of certainty. The *maturity* or life of the loan is usually short term (less than a year). From the lender's viewpoint, these characteristics offset the lack of collateral. (Grants and contract receivables can rarely be assigned.) From the point of view of the borrower, as long as the activities contracted under the grant can be carried out satisfactorily, there is little risk that the source of repayment will not come through as expected.

Bridge Financing

This type of financing need is similar to cash flow, but the *bridge* usually implies that a loan will be taken out, or refinanced, by another loan. For example, a nonprofit development organization might assemble a financing package for a real estate project which includes construction and permanent financing (i.e., a mortgage). The organization might utilize bridge financing to acquire the property that it will eventually develop. Repayment of the bridge loan would come at the time that the construction loan was *drawn down* or disbursed, or it might come at the closing of the permanent financing. In order to evaluate the risk of this loan, a lender would attempt to verify the completeness and certainty of the financial package. The loan is only considered a bridge loan if the refinancing can be relied upon.

Mortgage or Permanent Financing

This type of financing is utilized to acquire real property (i.e., a building). It is usually long term (at least five to ten years), and the source of repayment is either from the rental payments of tenants, from the revenue stream of the owner-occupant, or a combination thereof. By definition, a mortgage implies a security interest in the property. This offsets in the lender's mind the risks implied by the length of the term and the relative uncertainty of the revenue stream. Because most owners and tenants have some history of rental payments and occupancy expenses, it is fairly easy to evaluate the likelihood of repayment by comparing what the occupants are currently paying to what they would have to pay in order to support debt service (principal and interest payments).

The reluctance of lenders to make mortgage loans is often due to interest rate risk (the risk that they may lock themselves into a rate that is lower than their future cost of funds) rather than to credit risk (the risk of losing principal). Many lenders are also reluctant to make mortgage loans to nonprofits because it is politically difficult to foreclose if the organization defaults.

From the borrower's point of view, the risk associated with this type of loan is related to the ability of the lender to foreclose on real property, interest rate fluctuations (if it is not a fixed-rate loan), and the difficulty of obtaining a mortgage of a sufficiently long term so that debt service is affordable.

Construction Financing

In some respects, loans made for construction financing resemble bridge loans, since the repayment of a construction loan almost always comes from refinancing with a mortgage. On the other hand, construction loans carry *project risk*, i.e., the risk that the construction may not be completed on time, within budget, or according to specifications. Construction lenders almost always require that the take out (permanent financing) be identified up front, but there is always the risk that the permanent financing will be withdrawn or the construction never completed. Some construction loans are structured to convert to permanent loans (mortgages) at the completion of construction.

From the borrower's point of view, the risk of a construction loan is primarily project risk—that funds will be inadequate, that completion will be delayed (causing interest expense to mount), and that permanent financing will evaporate.

Equipment Financing

This is, as it sounds, a financing secured by the equipment that is purchased with the loan proceeds. For example, a nonprofit publisher might utilize equipment financing to purchase word-processing equipment. This seems like a straightforward type of asset-based financing. But when the source and timing of repayment is considered, equipment financing takes on some of the risk characteristics of working capital. Like working capital, equipment financing is repaid by cash flows generated by the operations of the business. Because equipment financing is, by definition, utilized by manufacturing or service businesses, these cash flows are not highly predictable. While lenders will insist on securing themselves with the equipment (and generally will not lend for a term exceeding the life of the equipment), they do not expect to have to liquidate it to be repaid. Unlike real estate, equipment generally loses value over time due to physical decay or obsolescence. Additional value may be lost if the equipment has to be sold quickly.

Working Capital Financing

The term *working capital financing* sometimes carries different meanings. It is helpful to start with the accounting definition, which identifies working capital as the difference between current assets and current liabilities. (*Current* means that within one year the assets will convert to cash and the liabilities will have to be satisfied.)

Current assets could exceed current liabilities, however, and the business might still be short of cash to acquire inventory, meet payroll, or pay occupancy costs because current assets may include non-cash assets such as inventory and receivables. This situation is what a working capital loan is intended to cover. This situation frequently occurs when a business is expanding, and inventory and receivables are growing faster than the receivables are being collected. Although working capital is usually considered to be a short-term need, in practice it frequently takes many years for an enterprise to be able to generate sufficient cash from operations to repay a working capital loan. If the business continues to grow, it may never be able to repay a working capital loan. (Banks euphemistically call these loans "evergreen" credits. The loan is just rolled over every time it falls due.)

A working capital loan may also take the form of a *seasonal line of credit*, whereby inventory or receivables are financed during one season of the year, and repayment occurs during another season of the year as inventory is sold or as receivables are collected. For example, a museum gift shop might borrow under a seasonal line of credit during the fall in order to stock inventory for the Christmas selling season. Repayment of its borrowings would occur as inventory was sold.

Because working capital needs traditionally relate to the *timing* of cash inflows and outflows, working capital loans are frequently confused with cash flow loans. The important distinction, however, is that the existence of a source of repayment for the cash flow loan can be verified with some degree of certainty before the loan is made. For example, a youth employment and training organization receives a city contract that partially subsidizes the cost of its construction rehab unit. It borrows for its cash flow needs from a community foundation that operates a cash flow loan program. The manager of the loan fund can call the city official responsible for the contract, and verify the amount and timing of the contract receivable. The repayment of a working capital loan, however, depends on the production, marketing, and distribution of a product. How successfully this will occur cannot be predicted with certainty.

Because the source of repayment is relatively unpredictable, and because collateral (if available) is difficult to assign, monitor, or liquidate, lenders view working capital loans as extremely high risk. As with equipment financing, collateral of some kind will often be taken, but the expectation is that it will not have to be liquidated to repay the loan. From the borrower's point of view, the risk associated with a working capital loan is the risk that the business will not generate sufficient cash when needed to service debt when it comes due and, to the extent that assets of the business are assigned as collateral, that the lender will take control of those assets.

Seed Capital

Seed capital is often confused with working capital. In this chapter, it is used to describe the funds that are used to start an enterprise. Seed capital is what must be invested even before the enterprise reaches the stage where working capital can be applied. Seed capital might be used to do a feasibility study, to carry out test marketing, or to acquire equipment. It bears the very highest risk of all, because it must be obtained before there is any evidence that the business is viable. Unlike the other types of financing described above, seed capital can rarely be obtained in the form of a loan. The primary risk to the funder is that the enterprise will never materialize, revenues will never be generated, no return will be available, and there is no way of recovering the investment.

OBSERVATIONS

The nonprofit entrepreneur will have the risk factors associated with his enterprise pointed out to him as he "shops" his business plan around to financial institutions. In large measure, the type of venture he chooses determines the kind or kinds of financing available to him. However, by identifying the risk factors in a systematic way, *before* approaching potential funding sources, the entrepreneur can make the process of searching for funds more efficient. Moreover, by identifying the risk *to the enterprise* associated with the various types of financing, many of the problems that may later develop as the result of an inappropriate financial package can be avoided. The following examples illustrate how one nonprofit used risk analysis to identify the types of financing appropriate for its venture.

WeatherRite Services, Inc. (a pseudonym) is a nonprofit that provides technical assistance in weatherization techniques to managers of both nonprofit and for-profit housing management companies. It has been in operation for two years. The agency derives a portion of its income from a contract with the municipal department of housing to provide consulting services to nonprofit housing managers. The contract is for one year, but the funds are not disbursed until the year is halfway over. Anticipating a cash flow shortfall, the organization looks for a cash flow loan to cover operating expenses until disbursement of the funds from the contract.

· In this example, the financial risk is modest. Although it is a service business, and therefore unable to offer collateral, the weatherization enterprise is two years old and thus can demonstrate a track record. The financial need relates to timing of a contract receivable, and the source of repayment is identifiable, predictable, and receivable within a short term (six months). In this case, a commercial bank would be an appropriate source of financing.

Suppose that the nonprofit decides to expand the for-profit side of its business. It hires another staff person to provide weatherization consulting services to for-profit landlords. It will be a year or two before sufficient consulting revenue is generated to cover the complete costs of the additional staff member and overhead. In this case, working capital is needed to cover the shortfall. This financial need is fundamentally different than the one to cover a contract payment anticipated in six months. Here, revenues from the new consulting business cannot be predicted with as much certainty as the city contract, and depend entirely on the ability of the nonprofit to market its services. Financing under these circumstances carries a much higher risk, and a more flexible source of financing, such as a program-related investment or grant, is appropriate.

FINANCING SOURCES AND INSTRUMENTS

The preceding section shows how risk level is linked to the nature of the enterprise, the track record of the enterprise, and the type of financing that is needed. This section will look at how to match the risk characteristics or risk profile of the enterprise to the various sources of financing available to the nonprofit enterprise. It identifies the financial instruments available from each source, the degree of risk accepted, and the level of return required, as well as the organizational implications, or risk to the borrower, of various types of financial relationships. Again, it is important to note that for many types of financial *need*, there are very few sources available. For example, it is much easier to locate sources of cash flow, construction, or mortgage financing than it is to identify seed or working capital.

Figure 1 illustrates the relationship between sources of financing available to nonprofit ventures and the risk factors identified in the preceding section. The X-axis represents risk level, in *descending* order of risk, according to the type of financing needed. On the Y-axis are some of the most frequently used sources of financing, listed in *ascending* order of aversion to risk. The curve illustrates the most likely match between source and risk profile.

Figure 2 highlights one of the unique features of nonprofit finance: the inverse relationship between risk and return. In conventional financial markets, high risk is usually associated with high return. For example, venture capital investors expect to receive a 30–40 percent return on their investment, because they are providing high-risk funds: seed or working capital. This financing may take the form of an equity investment in the business. In nonprofit finance, however, the sources that usually provide the equivalent of equity capital—boards of directors, friends of the organiza-

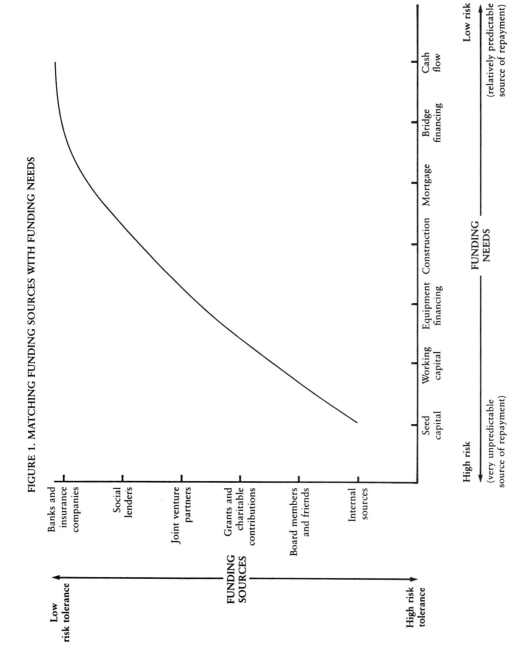

FIGURE 1. MATCHING FUNDING SOURCES WITH FUNDING NEEDS

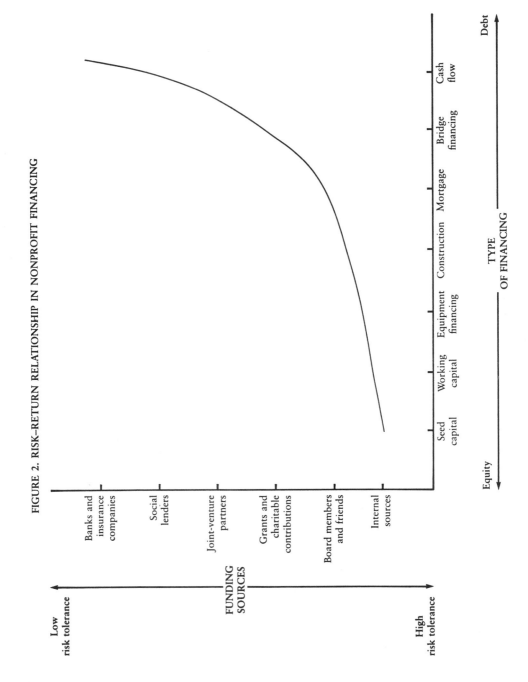

FIGURE 2. RISK–RETURN RELATIONSHIP IN NONPROFIT FINANCING

tion, charitable donations, or foundation grants—tend to be interested at least as much in the programmatic or charitable achievements of the venture. They are not looking for a high *financial* return. Thus, Figure 2 indicates that the return levels associated with high risk sources are the lowest; the return level associated with bank-and-insurance-company lending is the highest, even though the tolerance of risk by these sources is low.

SOURCES OF FINANCING

Internally Generated Funds

Unrestricted funds are the most flexible source of financing available to the nonprofit venture, and probably the most difficult to accumulate in large amounts. Internally generated funds include operating surplus from prior years, excess equipment and supplies, and staff time that is not needed for current activities of the organization. Internally generated funds are rarely available on a large scale, but frequently can be utilized in small amounts for seed capital purposes. For example, in the weatherization business example in the preceding section, the most appropriate source of funds for the costs of starting up the for-profit component of the consulting business would be internally generated funds. Because internally generated funds are so scarce, staff and boards of nonprofits need to weigh the risks of using these funds very carefully.

Board and Friends

These are good sources for seed and working capital. They are patient sources and willing to accept high risk. Although financing from board members may be structured as debt, the terms are usually more flexible than conventional debt would be. For example, a nonprofit agency that provides services to children with learning disabilities received a ten-year, no-interest loan from a board member to develop and market a line of games for children. Furthermore, wealthy board members and friends can sometimes serve as guarantors for debt that would otherwise be undercollateralized, such as a working capital loan from a bank. Because board members are being asked to commit their personal wealth, it is important for them (and they will expect) to be as familiar with the operations of the venture as a conventional lender would be, perhaps more so. This commitment implies a much more active involvement in day-to-day activities on the part of board members than most nonprofits are accustomed to, and usually requires adjustments on the part of board and staff.

Grants and Charitable Contributions

These sources have many of the characteristics of internal and board funding, and are also appropriate sources for seed and working capital. Unfortunately, many foundations prefer to support the costs of feasibility studies, rather than invest or lend start-up operating funds. They fear that if the venture does not meet its financial projections, they will be asked to increase their participation.

A foundation will occasionally make a recoverable grant for a market study or feasibility analysis, which will be recoverable in the event that the project succeeds financially, but which carries no penalties if it is not repaid. Grants for ventures are rarely available in large amounts, and many funders place restrictions on the use of grants for equipment, fixtures, or capital improvements. Charitable institutions usually have a clearly articulated, programmatic agenda, and it is important to make sure that the financial goals of the venture are not in conflict with the purpose of the grant as perceived by the grant-making institution.

For example, a nonprofit housing developer received a recoverable grant to acquire some properties for rehabilitation and resale to low-income families. The developer found that the only way that the project could repay the grant was if the houses were sold to upper-income families. Since the charitable goals of the project were very important to both parties, the developer was able to convince the foundation to make a traditional grant to the project.

Joint Venture Partners

Not all nonprofit ventures have for-profit partners, but where a co-venture makes sense, the for-profit partner is frequently a good source of seed capital and initial working capital. Joint ventures are probably most often seen in real estate development. For-profit developers are attracted by what the nonprofit organization can bring to the table: knowledge of and political clout in a community, tax benefits of depreciation and interest expense that the nonprofit can't utilize, and access to low-cost public and private sources of financing such as UDAGs, CDBG funds, or social investment loans. In addition to its real estate development expertise, credibility, and contacts with conventional sources of financing, the for-profit developer can provide funds to support the costs of feasibility analysis, preliminary architectural work, and marketing studies. Funds for these purposes are comparable to seed capital for a manufacturing or service business.

Joint venture partners are a good source of high-risk financing because they may be able to provide their own internally generated funds, they may be able to borrow at more favorable terms than their nonprofit partners, and, since they will be deriving financial benefits from the venture, it is reasonable to expect them to make an equity investment in it. Because for-profit venture partners do not place the same priority on the charitable goals of the nonprofit organization or its venture, it is important to make a careful analysis of the trade-offs between the value of their investment and the amount of control they will have over project operations.

For example, a nonprofit educational organization developed its own line of software for high school students. It entered into a joint venture agreement with a for-profit publisher, which agreed to pay for some of the development costs of the software as well as the cost of marketing and distribution. Knowing that its partner would put greater emphasis on the higher-margin, but least-educational products, the nonprofit made sure that the joint venture agreement specified that the publisher would market the complete software line for the first three years of the venture.

Social Lenders

Included in the social lending arena are, among others, community loan funds, foundation program-related investments,[1] and the social investment divisions of insurance companies. These so-called soft loans are made at much higher risk than conventional bank or insurance company loans. In practice, however, the types of financing social lenders provide are rarely available for seed- or working capital-financing needs. This is due not only to the moderate level of risk that social lenders are willing to assume, but also to the fact that social lenders, like their conventional counterparts, are usually unwilling to provide "patient capital."

Social investment loans are more likely to be available for equipment finance, construction, bridge and cash flow finance, and, occasionally (primarily from insurance companies), mortgages. To the extent that social lending is considered "soft" money, it is due to the willingness of the social lender to accept subordinated positions on collateral, to lend with less collateral than would normally be required, to defer payment for one or more years, and to offer a lower-than-market interest rate.

Social lenders, like their conventional lending counterparts, commonly expect a sophisticated business plan and will usually require loan documentation that is comparable to that of conventional lenders. Moreover, because social lenders have charitable objectives, there will generally be more restrictions on the use of the funds than there would be from a conventional lender. For example, a social lender that provided construction financing for a community development organization to build a small business incubator might place restrictions on the types of tenants who are eligible to lease space.

It is very important for the management of a nonprofit venture to make sure that they share the same view of the charitable purposes of the venture as the social lender, and that the need to generate profits from the venture does not compromise these programmatic objectives.

For example, a youth employment and training agency has a bulk food-processing subsidiary, whose purpose is to provide job-training slots for unemployed youths. The need to repay its equipment financing loan, however, has forced the business to cut labor costs and trim its staff, thus reducing its ability to carry out the social purpose for which the loan was made. The reverse may also occur: in this example, the social loan might have mandated that a certain number of training slots be maintained, and the cost of training may undermine the ability of the business to break even or earn a profit.

Banks and Insurance Companies

Banks are most comfortable at the low-risk end of the spectrum, with cash flow and bridge loans, construction and mortgage loans, and occasional equipment financing. Banks tend to be averse to risk because: 1) they are highly regulated and monitored by

---

[1]Program-related investments (PRIs) are loans, guarantees of loans, or equity investments in projects that serve social purposes. A PRI made by a foundation is subject to the same legal constraints as a grant and must conform to certain additional provisions of the Internal Revenue Code.

the comptroller of the currency in order to protect depositors, and 2) their potential loss, if a loan goes bad, is the entire loan balance, while their potential gain, as a percent of loan principal, is very small—often less than 1 percent after transaction costs and overhead are deducted. Because their margins are so thin, banks depend on volume to generate an adequate return on investment. For this reason, the small size of the loans needed by nonprofit ventures can be a problem as well. The transaction costs of making these small loans may make them unprofitable. Branch banks and community banks will frequently consider loans that are considered too small by the larger banks or by the main office. Because in insurance companies the investment function is usually centralized, and there is no branch banking function, small loans are rarely available. However, insurance companies will often provide a much longer term than will a bank, and are a good source of mortgage financing.

Banks probably have the greatest array of financial instruments. In addition to mortgages, construction loans, and bridge and cash flow loans, banks can make term loans (loans that amortize over a number of years), and offer lines of credit (informal borrowing relationships with or without loan documentation) and revolving credit lines (lines of credit that can be drawn down, repaid, and drawn down again). The different financial instruments imply different degrees of control for the bank. Control is exercised via the legal documentation (i.e., loan agreement, collateral assignment), the obligation of the bank to make funds available, and the terms of repayment.

For example, a line of credit has minimal legal documentation (frequently a letter agreement is all that is used) but the line is only a "moral obligation" on the part of the bank. The availability of funds under the line may be curtailed if the bank thinks the borrower's financial condition is shaky. Borrowings are made under demand notes, which may be called in at any time. Lines of credit may require a "clean-up period" during which all borrowings must be repaid. They are usually only issued for one-year periods and must be renewed. This is why lines of credit may not be suitable for non-seasonal working capital purposes, when the cash flow for repayment will only be available over an extended period.

FINANCING THE NONPROFIT VENTURE—KEY STEPS IN THE PROCESS

This section outlines the series of steps that the nonprofit entrepreneur needs to take as financing is sought for the enterprise. In broad terms, these are as follows:

1. Assessment of organizational capacity, appropriateness of the enterprise/industry to that capacity, effect of the enterprise on the charitable goals of the organization, margin and market analysis, pilot phase, or test market.
2. Development of financial projections, including break-even analysis and cash flow projections. Evaluation of riskiness of enterprise. Identification of financial *needs* and appropriate sources of financing.
3. Preparation of business plan. Approach and presentation to funding sources.

4. Response to criticism. Modification of business plan.

In order to illustrate its key points, this section will take a hypothetical nonprofit venture through the sequence of steps. Newtown Community Development Corporation (the CDC) serves a deteriorating ethnic neighborhood of a moderate-sized New England city.

The CDC has been providing social services for fifteen years. Services include employment training for youth and other hard-to-employ populations, high school equivalency training, instruction in English as a second language, day care, and substance abuse counseling. The CDC has also developed 200 units of low- and moderate-income housing for families and for the elderly. Because the ethnic community that it serves does not speak English as its native language, all of the CDC's programs are provided by a bilingual staff.

Since it developed its first housing project for the elderly five years ago, the CDC has been aware of a need in its community for long-term health care services that are suited to the needs of a low-income, non-English-speaking elderly population. A long-term care facility or nursing home that was especially adapted to the needs of this population would, the CDC believed, fill a significant gap in the social service network, which it was the CDC's mission to provide. Moreover, the facility would be not only a source of jobs for community residents, but also a site where the CDC could offer training in entry-level health care professions. This training would benefit the hard-to-employ population that the CDC had been serving since it was organized. The CDC went through a series of stages in the development of this venture, which are described in the following paragraphs.

1. Assessing organizational capacity. Appropriateness of the enterprise/industry to that capacity. Effect of the enterprise on the charitable goals of the organization. Margin and market analysis. Pilot phase or test market.

The goal of acquiring a long-term care facility emerged from Newtown CDC's yearly long-range planning retreat. The board and staff of the CDC looked at the organization's strengths—social service delivery, employment training, and real estate development—and its institutional mission. It viewed health care delivery for the elderly as a way of fulfilling multiple goals, and it saw ownership of the long-term care facility as being in keeping with the organizational strengths of the CDC. It put together a team, consisting of a staff person with employment training responsibilities, a staff person with real estate investment skills, and the president of the CDC, to begin to analyze the industry and look for investment opportunities.

One of the organizational capacity issues most frequently cited by funders is the need for someone in the nonprofit who has the time and the ability to pull information together, analyze it, package it in a business plan, and follow up the plan with potential funders. Although consultants can be very helpful, it is important for the nonprofit to identify staff who can take the lead in the development of the business plan and see the venture through to completion. Ideally, the person who will ultimately be responsible for managing the enterprise should also be involved in the development of the business plan. Senior management should be as familiar with the business plan as staff, and if possible, be involved from the beginning in its development. Since it is frequently responsible for making contacts with sources of funding, senior management should be able to respond to questions about the details of the plan.

One of the tasks with which the team was charged was to identify the management skills that would be needed to operate the facility. An important finding that the team made early in its investigations was that most nonprofit nursing homes hired licensed administrators, who were frequently under contract from a private firm specializing in this type of management. Thus, the role of the CDC would be to set policy for the administrator, develop an employment training program, and oversee the fulfillment of the charitable goals of the facility. Because the CDC would not have to be involved in the day-to-day management of the facility, the team felt comfortable with the "fit" between the CDC's capacity and the functions it would have to perform. These functions would not be a drain on the organization's staff and funding resources.

As the team began to investigate the nursing home industry, it quickly realized that this would not be an enterprise that could generate extra income for the CDC. Although many nursing homes are operated at a profit by private corporations, the low-income clientele that the CDC intended to serve would limit the profit margins that this enterprise could hope to realize. Therefore, as it proceeded with its plans, Newtown CDC was careful to make it clear to its board and to potential funders that the kind of enterprise it had in mind would fulfill charitable goals but would not contribute income to the parent organization.

One of the most important early-stage activities that the nonprofit entrepreneur can undertake is an analysis of the prevailing profit margins and market potential for the enterprise. Obtaining comparable data, especially for small enterprises, can be difficult. But it is occasionally possible to estimate margins by looking at the price of the goods or service(s), and inferring what the costs of labor, materials, and overhead are. For industries in which there are many competitors, industry reports such as Standard and Poor's can be helpful. Nonprofits, like for-profit entrepreneurs, need to ask whether this is a good business to get into, from a profit point of view. They need to identify the factors to which the margins in this business are sensitive, e.g., rising labor or materials costs, or pricing pressures from existing competition. They need to consider whether there is anything about the nonprofit nature of the enterprise that will make it either easier or more difficult to compete with more conventional operations.

For example, the Newtown CDC knew that the low-income population it wanted to serve, and the employment and training component of the project, would put pressure on the profit margins of the nursing home. On the other hand, the research team's investigations showed that the uniqueness of a culturally sensitive, bilingual facility would enhance its attractiveness to its constituency, virtually guaranteeing that every bed would be occupied. Since its objectives for the enterprise were to break even financially, not to generate revenues for the CDC, the special characteristics of the nonprofit did not make the enterprise less attractive to them. However, they realized that some additional funding might be needed in order to carry out the employment training objectives.

For those enterprises that lend themselves to a pilot phase or test market, these activities can be enormously helpful, both in guiding the development of the business plan and in convincing funders that the venture will succeed. Because running a pilot long-term care facility was not a viable option, the Newtown CDC decided to hire a health care marketing consultant to help them survey neighborhood residents, hospitals who refer patients, and others providing services to the elderly, in order to determine the demand for the proposed facility.

The CDC obtained a small amount of seed capital in the form of a grant from a local foundation. This enabled them to hire the consultant to conduct the market survey and analyze the feasibility of buying—as opposed to constructing—a facility. Following a lead generated by their research, the CDC learned that a sectarian-affiliated nursing home in the Newtown neighborhood was going to be put up for sale. The CDC contacted the management and board of the nursing home and entered into negotiations for the purchase of the facility. The owners of the nursing home and the CDC eventually reached agreement on a sales price for the facility, and signed a nonbinding agreement for the purchase. The agreement provided for the transfer of the property to the CDC over a two-year period, during which the CDC management would assume control and the existing patients would transfer to a new facility.

At this stage, the Newtown CDC development team knew that the next steps would be to develop financial projections for the facility, and to identify the amount and type of financing that would be needed to purchase and operate the facility.

2. Development of financial projections, including break-even analysis and cash flow projections. Evaluation of riskiness of enterprise. Identification of financial needs and appropriate sources of financing.

The development of financial projections is an extension of the margin and market analysis, and pilot or test market phase described above. For example, Newtown CDC took the local market data it had gathered, what it had learned about the margins prevailing in the industry, and the historical operating statements for the facility, then used this information to prepare projections of revenue and expense. It based these projections on assumptions about how many beds would be available, what the mix of higher revenue, private-pay, and lower revenue, publicly subsidized patients would be, and what the variable and fixed costs of operating the facility would be. It prepared several sets of income and expense projections, using both optimistic and pessimistic assumptions. Since Newtown CDC's objective was to serve a low-income population, it was interested in seeing whether it could operate the facility at a break-even level if as many as 90 percent of the patients received public subsidy. This projection represented a worst-case scenario from a financial point of view, but the best case from a charitable point of view.

In addition to income and expense projections, entrepreneurs and funders need to look closely at the break-even analysis for a new venture. Break-even can be expressed in terms of either the number of units that need to be sold or the revenues that need to be received in order for the enterprise to cover both its fixed and its variable costs. (For an explanation of how to calculate break-even, please see the *Business Planning Guide*, listed at the end of this book.) There are three key questions that managers and funders ask about break-even:

- What level of sales/units are needed in order to break even?
- How close is the enterprise to reaching that point?
- How will the business survive in the meantime?

For example, a nonprofit manufacturer of a children's toy calculated that it would take sales of 100,000 units of toys to cover fixed and variable costs of manufacturing and marketing the toy. Starting with its current sales level and projecting a steady annual sales-growth rate, the manufacturer projects that it will take five years to reach break-even. The manager of this venture realizes that no financing could be repaid before five years. The manager would also need to plan for how the business will cover its operating losses over the next five years.

Newtown CDC performed its break-even analysis to show at what occupancy rates its facility would cover all of its costs. It reasoned that during the first two years of ownership, the facility would average only 50 percent occupancy. In the third year, it would reach 75 percent occupancy, and would break even. In the fourth year, it would be able to generate a small operating surplus, which could be used to service debt. But the costs of providing the employment training to health care providers would not be covered for many years.

Newtown CDC prepared income, expense, and cash flow projections. The income and expense projections included non-cash expenses such as depreciation on the physical plant. The cash flow projections were based on the income and expense projections, but they were adjusted to reflect only the *cash* expenses as well as the *timing* of cash receipts and disbursements. As they developed their projections, staff members of Newtown CDC were careful to separate the ongoing cash flows related to operations from the cash flows related to start-up costs and purchase of the facility. They were therefore able to identify the following three distinct types of financing needs:

- Acquisition costs of the physical plant. These amounted to $1,000,000.
- Working capital needed to operate the facility until its third year, when it would break even. This amounted to $75,000 in the first year and $25,000 in the second year.
- Costs of operating the employment training component of the project. These included the costs of an instructor and a small stipend to the trainees, and amounted to approximately $35,000 per year.

At this point, the Newtown CDC development team was ready to build a risk profile for this project. They identified the risk characteristics of the venture and came up with the risk profile that follows.

Type of enterprise. The venture is a service business, and therefore relatively risky. The margins are thin, due in part to the charitable objectives of the enterprise. Offsetting this risk, however, is the marketing advantage associated with the bilingual, bicultural nature of the enterprise.

Track record. Although there is a track record for the existing operation, the facility will be operated by new management after it is sold to Newtown CDC. This will be a new type of enterprise for Newtown CDC, and therefore it carries the high-risk characteristics of a start-up venture. However, the CDC is experienced in providing social services to the elderly. Moreover, the CDC will contract with an experienced nursing home operator to manage the day-to-day operations of the facility, and this operator will be phased in over two years, thus providing for a smooth transition between existing and new management. These factors offset somewhat the lack of experience of the CDC in this venture.

Type of financing needed. Three types of financing needs were identified as a result of preparing the financial projections. For each one, the development team considered the purpose of the required financing, the availability of collateral, the predictability of the source of repayment, and the amount of time it would take to repay it.

Acquisition financing—In order to purchase the facility, the CDC would need to obtain a twenty-year mortgage. The mortgage would be secured by the underlying real estate, which was appraised at $1.2 million. The existing operation had always been able to service a mortgage from its operating revenues, although the interest rate had been lower than the current rates available from banks. The chief risk to a mortgage lender would thus be whether the new operation could generate cash flows that were at least as good as those generated by the existing operation. The CDC development team judged that, given the collateral and the relatively predictable cash flows, this type of financing reflected only moderate risk to a lender, and that a bank would be an appropriate source of financing.

Working capital financing—This type of financial need represented a much higher risk than mortgage financing. There was no security available for this financing, and even though working capital was only needed for two years, the financial projections indicated that it would be many years before it could be repaid, if ever. The development team thought that it would make sense to seek a combination of soft loans and grant funding for working capital.

Employment training costs—There was little likelihood that the operations of the nursing home itself would ever generate sufficient funds to cover these costs. These costs represented the riskiest component of the financial projections, but had the closest association to the charitable goals of the project. The CDC team considered several charitable sources for these funds.

As it reviewed the risk profile that it had developed for the project, the Newtown CDC development team realized that it needed to seek funding for the different financing needs of the long-term care facility from several sources. For the relatively low-risk acquisition financing, it would approach a bank that had financed its previous real estate projects. It would approach a combination of foundations and board members for grants and no-interest, long-term loans for the $100,000 in working capital. And it would use internally generated funds and apply for public sector contracts for the employment training activities. At this stage, Newtown CDC was ready to take its business plan to potential financing sources.

3. Preparation of business plan. Approach and presentation to funding sources.

The business plan serves two important functions. First, it is a kind of road map for management of an enterprise. It lays out a plan of action for the first few years of the life of the enterprise, and serves as a reference point against which the actual experience of the venture can be compared. Business plans are often adjusted as the underlying assumptions are tested against reality.

The second function that a business plan performs is as a supporting document, which assists management to attract financing for the venture. It is important to note that the business plan is really just a *supporting* document—if funders do not have confidence in management's ability to carry out its objectives, it will not matter how impressive the business plan looks. However, a well-reasoned and well-presented plan is a strategic tool that can play an important role in securing financing for a venture. The financial projections contained in the business plan identify the amount and timing of financing needed to make the venture work as well as the amount and timing of cash available to repay debt or recover equity investment. The marketing, management, and operating information included in the plan provide support for the financial projections.

Funders look for ways to support or challenge the assumptions used in the financial projections. If the people who prepared them are experienced in the particular business, the assumptions take on an added credibility. Funders want to know that assumptions can be documented through experience or, at worst, through market sampling. They are also interested in management's ability to learn from past mistakes and to adapt to change. Thus, management's ability to fulfill past projections of performance, whether with this venture or a related activity, will be taken into consideration.

Newtown CDC chose to approach the bank from which it had borrowed previously, because this bank was familiar with Newtown CDC management and the CDC had developed a good credit history with the bank. In addition, the president of the CDC sat on the community affairs advisory board of the bank. So, for its initial contact, the CDC had its real estate development staff person contact the bank, submit the business plan, and arrange a follow-up meeting with the loan officer and the CDC president.

Nonprofits without previous borrowing experience are often able to establish borrowing relationships with banks that maintain the nonprofit's operating accounts. If the operating relationship is a substantial one, it is probably highly profitable to the bank and can be used as leverage to obtain credit with the bank. Frequently, board members can help to obtain entry to banks where their businesses have operating or credit relationships.

As the Newtown CDC development team worked on the business plan, it kept in mind that the bank would be looking for thoroughness, accuracy, and a realistic, objective tone. They knew that the tone of the business plan is an important signal to funders. If there is a great deal of promotion relative to substantive information, funders will lose interest. They have to discount so much of what is said that they end up discounting the entire package. On the other hand, the development team knew that nothing is as comforting to funders as a plan that demonstrates an awareness of (and preparation for) potential problems. It indicates to them that the people who have developed the venture have a realistic view of what it takes to be successful. Therefore, they included both optimistic and pessimistic projections for five years, which showed that a twenty-year mortgage could be serviced even under worst-case conditions.

The CDC development team also included plenty of back-up information, in particular the assumptions used in making the financial projections. The data that it had obtained during the market survey stage were especially helpful, as were the operating statements of the prior owners of the facility. They expected that the bank's loan officer would compare the financial projections with the previous operating history, and with the operating margins that were prevalent in the industry.

Although they intended to use the same business plan in their approach to other sources of funding, the CDC development team members decided to deemphasize the employment training goals in their presentation to the bank, and add an additional section to the plan when they submitted it to foundations and board members for working capital financing. They were prepared, however, to discuss with the bank the reasons why it was important for the facility to serve a low-income clientele, even though that would mean that margins and debt service coverage would be thin.

As they prepared for the meeting with the bank, the president of the CDC and the real estate investment staff person tried to think of the kinds of questions that the loan officer would ask. They knew that the loan officer would try to challenge the financial projections. In particular, they expected that they would be asked to defend the assumptions underlying their projections of income and expense, since these differed from those of the previous operation. In anticipation of questions about this, they prepared a comparison of their projections and the historical statements, which showed the reasons for the differences between the two operations. They also expected to be asked about the sources of working capital for the first two years, and therefore obtained letters of support from two board members and a foundation who were considering requests from Newtown CDC.

The CDC development team knew that the bank would ask about management for the long-term care facility. While the CDC couldn't sign a contract with an administrator until it had obtained financing for the purchase, it had identified two management firms that it felt could do the job. The team prepared a briefing packet about these firms' capabilities, including a list of similar facilities under their management.

Having received the business plan well in advance of the meeting, the loan officer of the bank was familiar with the details of the plan. During the meeting, he told the representatives of the CDC that his chief concern was with the thin debt service coverage during the early years of the venture. Although he realized that the working capital financing, which the CDC would obtain, would include the first two years of debt service, he was worried about the possibility that the operation might not meet its operating projections. If break-even did not occur until year five or six, there might not be sufficient cash flow to service the loan. Although the venture offered good collateral in the form of a security interest in the land and building, the banker knew that his bank would find it extremely difficult to foreclose on the property because the borrower was a charitable institution.

The president of the CDC and his associates felt discouraged by the banker's reaction to their business plan. They knew that their financial projections were conservative and that there was sufficient cash flow to service the loan. However, they also knew that it was important not to react defensively in the meeting. They listened to the banker's concerns, and told him that they would try to find a way to provide an additional cash flow cushion to the project. Before leaving the meeting, they fixed a date for a follow-up meeting with the banker, at which they would present their ideas.

4. Response to criticism. Modification of business plan.

Funders of nonprofit ventures pay close attention to how managers respond to their concerns. They are assessing how responsive management is going to be to obstacles and challenges. If a manager responds inflexibly to criticism about his or her business plan, that is an indication that he or she may fail to modify plans and assumptions in the face of actual experience in the marketplace. Funders place more confidence in managers who turn challenges and criticism into an opportunity to improve their business plans and their enterprises.

When the Newtown CDC returned to the bank, they presented a plan that they thought would alleviate the bank's concerns, and also strengthen the project. They had used the intervening time to approach a community foundation for assistance. The community foundation had agreed to place an interest-bearing deposit with the bank for six years. While the principal of the deposit would not be pledged to the bank, the interest on the deposit would be available to the bank for debt service in case of a cash flow shortfall in the facility. Any funds not needed for debt service on the loan would be placed in a special fund for the benefit of the employment training component of the project. The banker responded positively to this plan, and the Newtown CDC was able to successfully conclude negotiations for the mortgage loan.

GENERAL OBSERVATIONS

The Newtown CDC was successful in its search for financing for the acquisition of the long-term care facility. It may be helpful to summarize the factors which contributed to its success.

1. Board and staff of the CDC considered the organizational capabilities of the CDC, and sought a venture opportunity that had a good fit with those capabilities.

2. The CDC looked at the market and margins for the type of business it wanted to operate, and tried to determine what positive and negative effect the nonprofit context would have on its operations.

3. The CDC developed financial projections under a variety of scenarios, in order to determine what the financing needs of the venture were under the most pessimistic conditions.

4. The CDC used its assessment of the financial needs, type of venture, and management experience available to the venture to evaluate the overall risk of the venture and determine what types of financial instruments were appropriate.

5. Because different components of the project carried different levels of financial risk, the CDC approached more than one type of financing source.

6. The CDC was able to hear the concerns of a potential lender and respond flexibly to those concerns.

7

Organizing for Business: The Organizational Context of Income-Generating Activities

WIM WIEWEL

BEFORE A NONPROFIT can deal with the question of the appropriate organizational structure for its business, it must clearly define the goals it seeks to pursue through enterprise. Only after the goals, the kind of venture, and competitive environment are precisely determined, should different organizational formats be investigated, and one selected. The "correct" organizational structure is thus a contextual matter, which cannot be settled purely in terms of theoretical or legalistic debate.

This chapter presents a decision-making system for choosing the proper organizational format for revenue-generating activities. It focuses on three key decisions: whether the new activity should be structured as a for-profit business or nonprofit program; whether it should be organized and run in-house or as a separate entity; and, if it is a separate entity, how much control and ownership the parent organization should keep. A final section discusses the critical "incubation period" during which time-organizational choices, as well as a host of other matters, can be worked out.

STRUCTURING INCOME-GENERATING ACTIVITIES

This section presents a decision-making process to help an organization plan and evaluate the organizational structure most appropriate for its new venture(s).[1]

The decision tree in Figure 1 presents three main choices regarding profit, separation, and extent of control. Each decision generally covers a unique set of concerns. The

[1]Much of this material appeared earlier in different form in *Business Spin-offs: Planning the Organizational Structure of Business Activities—A Manual for Not-for-Profit Organizations*, by Wim Wiewel, James Ridker, Robert Mier, and Robert Giloth, of the Center for Urban Economic Development, University of Illinois at Chicago, Chicago (1982).

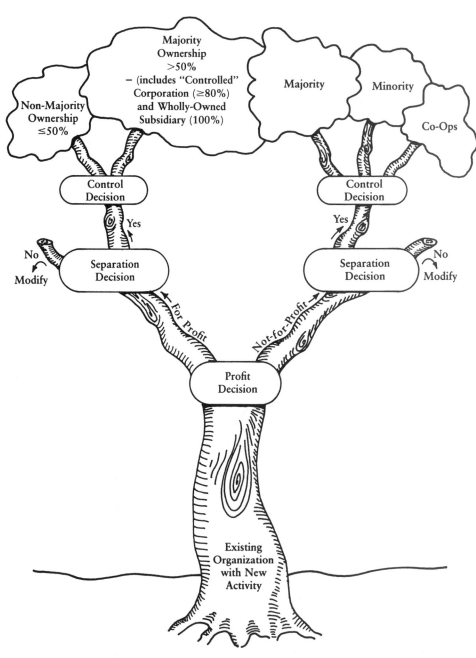

FIGURE 1. DECISION TREE

TABLE I. FOR-PROFIT OR NONPROFIT: ADVANTAGES AND DISADVANTAGES

	Advantages	Disadvantages
For-profit or un-related business activity	Access to capital Access to capital entrepreneurs Compensation Write off losses More freedom for operations Access to jobs	Tax liability False expectations Advantages of not-for-profit status are lost
Nonprofit or related business activity	Access to grants Designation as "related business activity" protects tax exemptions No tax liability More appeal to volunteer commitment	Uncertain tax status Advantages of for-profit are lost

profit decision analyzes the implications of operating the business on a for-profit basis or on a nonprofit basis. The *separation decision* asks the organization to consider whether an activity should be run in-house or as a separate entity. The *control decision* examines the consequences of varying degrees of control that the organization may have over an activity structured as a separate entity. Working through the decision tree will help the organization determine the structure that fits its needs.

For-Profit or Nonprofit?

In many cases, nonprofit organizations undertake revenue-generating activities which can be considered either for-profit ventures or nonprofit programs. Some programs may be new; others may have been in place for years. For example, programs may generate fees-for-service, or sales from the publication of materials, or income from the work of members or clients. At some point, senior staff or trustees, or both, may conclude that ongoing programs should be reevaluated for the appropriateness of their organizational structures, while new or contemplated programs should be started with the most effective structural design. See Table I for a comparison of the advantages and disadvantages of for-profit and nonprofit organizations.

Advantages of For-Profit or Unrelated Business Activity Status

Access to capital. A separate for-profit corporation may be better able to attract private investment capital than a program of a nonprofit. Capital can come from banks, corporations, "friends," and even members or employees. It can come in the form of equity investments or loans, or it can be facilitated by loan guarantees. Investors or lenders will be motivated by a desire for return on their investment and may provide management assistance as well. They may formally establish a joint venture with the nonprofit. For instance, The Woodlawn Organization (TWO) in Chicago entered into a separate for-profit partnership with Hillman, a food store chain, to develop the TWO-Hillman supermarket. Hillman provided the capital to build the store and the senior management; TWO, the labor and some of the capital. Of course, bringing in investors usually requires giving up some control, and certainly some of the profits, to the outside parties.

In making business loans, banks and other participants often prefer to deal with for-profit enterprises. A separate, for-profit enterprise fits their "model" of lending criteria and they understand their operations better. Moreover, banks do not want to be put in a position of foreclosing or calling in an investment in a charitable organization.

Access to entrepreneurs. Closely related to the previous point is the possibility of bringing in skilled management in a for-profit activity. In the example given above, Hillman manages the food store. Other arrangements may include financial counseling and systems design. Numerous studies of business success and failure suggest the crucial role of management, and if the nonprofit doesn't have it, or have it in depth, acquiring it in exchange for equity participation can make much sense.

Compensation. For-profits can provide numerous incentives to attract and hold valued employees. Equity participation, profit sharing, and sales bonuses, unavailable within a nonprofit legal structure, can motivate key workers and improve the business environment. At a minimum, the availability of compensation alternatives means a wider pool of potential employees will be available to the nonprofit entrepreneur.

Write-off of losses. Most new activities start out operating at a financial loss, which may continue for several years. Initial investments must be made, fixed costs may be high, and establishing a track record and attracting clientele can take time. Losses incurred during the first year(s) can be used by a for-profit business to offset profit in subsequent years, so that taxation may be avoided for several years. Operating losses can be carried forward. This tax provision applies to both for-profit subsidiaries and unrelated businesses carried on within a nonprofit organization.

Freedom to operate and grow. In general, there are fewer restrictions and clearer legal rulings regarding what for-profit corporations can do. If for-profit status is adopted, there are very few limits to the range of activities that can be undertaken, and no constraints on growth. This benefit accrues particularly to separate for-profit corporations, rather than to activities run as an unrelated business by a nonprofit.

Access to jobs, image, and respectability. Some business activity is open only to for-profit enterprises. For instance, Tri-City Citizens Union for Progress in New Jersey, a nonprofit organization, has been required by the Department of Housing and Urban Development (HUD) to work with for-profit companies in order to do housing projects. HUD assumed for-profit corporations would be more effective and efficient. This appears to be a problem of image rather than substance, since Tri-City has survived all the for-profit partners it has worked with so far. The city of Chicago recently changed its practices so that contracts for weatherization work are now available only to for-profit companies.

Further, communities and employees may derive a certain pride, and identity, by being connected with a for-profit company. The morale of staff may improve as well.

Disadvantages of For-Profit Status

Tax liability. A major disadvantage of a for-profit or unrelated business activity is its tax liability. Profits taken by the government leave less for program enhancement. Nevertheless, paying taxes is a small price to pay for a successful venture, and tax considerations are rarely the prime determinant in selecting the "correct" structure.

False expectations. In many low-income communities profit potential is limited, and forming a for-profit corporation does not change that. If a new for-profit fails to produce significant net earnings, the enthusiasm of personnel, board members, and the parent organization may rapidly dissipate, and the operations of the business may falter.

Advantages of nonprofit status are lost. The other disadvantages of for-profit status are the reverse of the advantages of nonprofit status detailed in the following section.

Advantages of Nonprofit or Related Business Activity Status

Access to grants and subsidies. A nonprofit entity has access to a variety of government grant programs and charitable funding from individuals, corporations, and foundations that are unavailable to a for-profit enterprise. These funds may be available on "softer" terms, for longer periods of time, and with fewer bottom-line requirements than if they came from the private sector. Moreover, while investment capital is theoretically available to for-profits, it may never materialize if the corporation's profit potential, or its track record, is limited. In such cases, staying nonprofit may be the most viable option.

Designation of "Related Business Activity." If the enterprise is structured so that it is substantially related to the organization's exempt purposes, it can do as much "business" as it chooses without paying an unrelated business income tax and will not have its tax exemption jeopardized. For example, in the late 1970s and early 1980s, the Denver Children's Museum earned more than 95 percent of its income, all related to its exempt purpose. Related activity protects exemption and minimizes challenges to exempt status.

No tax liability. An obvious advantage of carrying on activities under a nonprofit tax-exempt structure is that no federal tax liability is incurred. For instance, one East Coast community organization has operated a nonprofit janitorial services business for many years as a separate nonprofit corporation. Its goals, entitling it to tax exemption, are the training of unskilled workers and the alleviation of poverty. The company bids on jobs alongside regular commercial firms and sometimes wins. So far this arrangement has not been challenged.

Nonprofit businesses may have to pay local sales and property taxes, depending on the state or locality in which they operate.

More appeal to volunteer commitment. Nonprofit status enables an organization to use volunteers. This may not only lead to increased earned income, it may also help expand the programs of the organization. Indeed, the federal tax code encourages this form of participation by specifically exempting from tax enterprises that are operated with 80 percent or more volunteer labor.

Shared staff and resources. Nonprofit organizations can contribute staff and physical resources to increase the chances of success of earned income activities. Free or low-cost office space, equipment, and personnel, even part-time, cut expenses and, at the same time, enhance an understanding within the organization about how the income-earning program works.

Disadvantages of Nonprofit or Related Business Activity Status

Uncertain tax status. Whenever an activity is regularly carried on and generates income, its tax-exempt status may be challenged. Whether it is considered a related business activity of a parent nonprofit organization or is carried on by an independent nonprofit subsidiary, the Internal Revenue Service can always look further into the matter. Thus, the presence of nonprofit enterprise requires constant attention and caution, to make sure the activities continue to be substantially related to the tax-exempt purposes of the organization.

Nonprofits that do engage in unrelated business activity do not necessarily jeopardize their exempt status. A rule of thumb is that the organization can gross as much as 20–25 percent of its operating budget in unrelated income without serious concerns about its tax status. At the same time, it should declare the unrelated income and pay tax on it.

Advantages of for-profit status are lost. The other disadvantages of the nonprofit form are simply the reverse of the advantages of the for-profit format.

Separate Versus In-House: Pros and Cons

In developing a new activity or deciding the future of an ongoing one, the parent organization may be faced with the choice of running the activity in-house or establishing it as a separate entity. This separation decision must be made whether the activity is operated for charitable or for profit-making purposes. Organizations making this decision must balance their need to maintain direct control and nurture a young project against the need to create other options for management and limit risk exposure. Table II compares the advantages and disadvantages of separation and no separation.

Advantages of Separation

Focused program purpose. When an organization separates out its enterprise, the result can be a clearer focus of activities in both operations. Board and staff are attentive to one purpose. Priorities are not open to trade-offs and, thus, there may be

TABLE II. SEPARATION DECISION: ADVANTAGES AND DISADVANTAGES

	Advantages	Disadvantages
Separation	Focused program purpose Inspire confidence and credit Protect parent's tax-exemption and parent from liability Permit development of a new board	Loss of control Redundant use of resources Costs of forming a separate entity
No separation	Direct management and control Organizational and staff development Flexible use of personnel Safeguard community purpose Tax exemption more easily defended	Dilution of purpose Parent liability Jeopardy to parent's tax-exempt status

less competition for scarce resources. With fewer distractions, each operation may become more efficient.

Inspire confidence and credit. Separation confers a unique identity, which, if the enterprise is successful, can enhance the interest and confidence outside suppliers or financiers may have in the operation. Particularly if the new organization is a for-profit venture, banks and other lending institutions may feel more comfortable in dealing with the enterprise and perhaps be more responsive to its requests for infusions of cash. Furthermore, management talent may find the separation more congenial to their interests and more comfortable in terms of their working styles, and be more willing to seek employment.

Protect the organization's tax exemption. A separate organization will insulate its parent from challenges to its tax-exempt status and protect it from liability.

Permit development of a new board. The organization, by separating, can take certain of its most interested and talented board members and use them as the nucleus of a focused new board. In addition, new members with specific expertise in, say, marketing or finance or law, can be induced to serve on the board, thus strengthening it and improving its chance for success.

Advantages of Nonseparation

Direct management and control. Under this approach, the operation will be run in-house, probably as a program division of the organization. As such, control over the activity is direct, since no separate organizational structure intervenes in the decision-making and administrative processes. With short lines of authority, and close-in decision-making, policy or program conflicts can be minimized.

Organizational and staff development. Because the program is administratively close, staff members may gradually expand their range of involvements and possibly even take over new program areas. This option potentially offers new career paths for talented staff members desirous of promotion or advancement.

Flexible use of personnel. As a program division of the organization, various staff members may contribute on a part-time basis their skills in, say, marketing or finance. Since cash may be in short supply, this approach can conserve resources until the organization must hire new staff. Indeed, certain tasks may not need a full-time staff member and the organization can use one person to perform several functions.

Safeguard community purpose. The separation issue has a public relations aspect. Particularly if the organization is grass roots in nature, separation, especially as a for-profit entity, may suggest a kind of "selling out" to other interests. Indeed, the concern may be well founded, since, as a for-profit entity, community needs may not be of paramount concern.

Tax exemption is more easily defended. If the organization chooses not to separate out the new activity, it may well indicate to the community and the IRS its confidence in the knowledge that the activity is substantially related to the exempt mission.

To accommodate a new activity in-house, the board and senior staff may have to modify the existing organization. This may involve minor administrative changes or reformulating the whole scope of activity as stated in the articles of incorporation. This involves revising the bylaws and revamping the board structure.

Some organizations may choose to start the new activity as a program division, only later spinning it off as a separate nonprofit or for-profit entity. As the unit grows and takes shape, it may virtually demand separate treatment. Thus, separation may well be a developmental concern having both organizational and financial components. The following *organizational* indicators suggest the need to think about separation:

- There is a need to focus the board on the targeted activity.
- The board of the parent organization has become overburdened by the proliferation of programs or by programs with widely divergent needs.
- A program is unable to operate effectively because it is stigmatized by association with the parent.
- Programs are inefficiently competing for the use of staff and/or other shared resources.
- The work plan for the subsidiary activity is sufficiently developed so that staffing, cash flow, and other day-to-day issues can be reasonably projected to assure its viability as an independent entity.

The following *financial* indicators suggest the need to think about separation:

- Capital is needed that separation may attract.
- The creation of new options for ownership of a particular activity serves some goals of the organization. These options may include the creation of a cooperative, the bringing in of an entrepreneur, or the selling of stock interest in a specific activity to community residents or employees.
- The extent of the "unrelated" operations of an in-house activity threatens the non-profit status of the parent.

- There is substantial risk associated with an activity that could cause the parent to assume an excessive degree of liability.
- Separation provides tax advantages that would not otherwise be available.

Some of the most compelling arguments for separation may be financial. The IRS insists, however, that separation be based on organizational reasons, and not on the desire to gain tax advantages.

If only the organizational indicators call for some degree of separation, and fiscal matters are not at issue, separation may be achieved in-house, without the establishment of the activity as a completely independent entity. Managerial modifications of the parent organization can be made to achieve some degree of practical separation without creating a formal, legal separation. The program may be directed by a board committee, which is given substantial autonomy in its decision making. Staff may be kept separate except at the highest echelon. Various in-house programs may operate at different locations so that day-to-day contact among their staffs is limited. Any of these techniques may be used to achieve de facto separation as a method of increasing efficiency of operations and avoiding the problem of dilution of purpose.

A parent organization may exercise control over its subsidiary's operations and still preserve both of their separate legal identities as long as "the corporate veil" is not pierced. Essentially, the courts have held that the owners of a corporation (in this case, the parent organization that owns a subsidiary corporation) may be held liable when the corporate form is used to defraud, mislead, or confuse a third party, and where corporate formalities are neglected. Under such circumstances the third party may "pierce the corporate veil," that is, sue the parent for the actions of the subsidiary. (See the chapter by Bruce Hopkins for a more complete discussion of these points.)

Another concern is whether the IRS will regard the actual separation, in addition to the nominal separation, as sufficient to protect the parent's tax-exempt status.

The following list indicates the areas where it may be important to maintain strict separation between the parent and subsidiary:

- Avoidance of meddling in day-to-day affairs
- Separate bylaws that establish membership and voting
- Independent documentation (minutes of board proceedings, financial records, contracts)
- Clear delineation of responsibilities of personnel
- Adequate capitalization of subsidiary; separate bank account
- Business dealings of subsidiary not limited to providing services to parent
- Separate dealings with clients
- Subsidiary not held primarily responsible for the financial gain of the nonprofit parent.

If parent control cuts across too many of these areas—such as with overlapping boards and officers, control of finances, and control of operations—and an element of fraud or unfairness is present, the courts may hold the parent liable for the debts and obligations of the subsidiary.

TABLE III. ADVANTAGES AND DISADVANTAGES OF VARYING DEGREES OF OWNERSHIP

	Advantages	Disadvantages
Majority-owned (51–99%)	Retain control, but allow for input. If ownership is less than 80% parent is not taxed on payments received from subsidiary. If ownership is more than 80%, multiple subsidiaries may consolidate tax returns. (This may be done in a holding company.)	Multiple subsidiaries may not consolidate tax returns if parent has less than 80% ownership. Risk of stigma. Payments from subsidiary to parent are taxable; if more than 80% ownership.
Non-majority-owned (50% or less)	Create maximum options for input (entrepreneur, employees, community, parent); some control may be possible. Parent is not taxed on some payments received from subsidiary. Avoid stigma.	Parent may lack control.

By following some guidelines, a parent organization can have much latitude controlling the operations of its subsidiary. Principally, it must pay its taxes, avoid fraudulent behavior, and be able to demonstrate that the subsidiary is independently viable.

How Much Control?

If a nonprofit organization has decided to set up a separate organization to run a new activity, it must decide how much control it wants to retain. Control is the ability to influence the corporation's actions, usually based on stock ownership or the ability to make appointments to the board of directors.

This section focuses on the issues affecting the control of for-profit corporations. The control of in-house programs and of affiliate nonprofit organizations has been given consideration in the preceding section on separation. Table III summarizes the advantages and disadvantages of the varying degrees of ownership.

Control and taxation vary over the different ranges of ownership. Extent of control of a subsidiary is treated here in two broad categories only: majority-owned (51 or more percent ownership), and non-majority-owned (50 percent or less ownership). The non-majority-owned category includes the option of totally relinquishing control. Only the advantages of each of the two types will be discussed.

Advantages of Majority Ownership (51 percent or more)

Majority ownership exists when the parent controls more than half of the interest in the subsidiary. If ownership is 100 percent, the subsidiary is considered wholly owned and is completely controlled by the parent. If ownership is at least 80 percent, the subsidiary is considered a *controlled* corporation. Ownership of controlled corporations entitles a for-profit parent (or a holding company owned by the nonprofit community organization) to consolidate tax returns of those subsidiaries in which it has at least 80 percent ownership. If ownership is less than 80 percent, receipts of payments of rent or interest from the subsidiary are tax-exempt to the nonprofit parent.

Retention of Control, and Allowance for Input (51 percent or more). Less than 100 percent ownership provides an opportunity to introduce input from other sources. This could come in the form of capital from an entrepreneur, community ownership of stock, employee ownership of stock through an employee stock ownership plan, or representation on the board of directors by persons other than those appointed or elected by the parent organization. Of course, as long as the parent organization retains majority control the degree to which real input is sought and allowed remains at its discretion.

Consolidation of Tax Returns of Multiple Subsidiaries (80 percent or more). If an organization spins off multiple subsidiaries, some of which are profitable and others not, there may be an advantage to consolidating their tax returns. By consolidation, tax deductions such as losses, depreciation, and tax credits of one subsidiary offset the profits of another subsidiary of the parent so that tax liability is reduced. The IRS requires, in order to consolidate tax returns, that the parent organization and the subsidiaries be for-profit corporations. It further requires that each subsidiary be owned 80 percent or more by the same parent. If the parent organization is nonprofit, it may establish a holding company (a for-profit entity that the nonprofit parent can hold to whatever share of ownership it desires). The consolidated tax return reports the income and loss of the for-profit parent (or holding company) as well as that of the subsidiaries. Together they are called an *affiliated group*. Consolidation and establishment of the holding company, however, are not advantageous in all situations.

Some Payments from Subsidiary are Tax-Free for Parent Organization (less than 80 percent). A nonprofit organization does not have to pay taxes on dividends. Generally it is exempt from taxation on interest it receives, and on rental income from real property which it owns.[2] However, these exemptions do *not* apply to rents or interest received from a controlled organization. Thus, if a nonprofit organization owns 80 percent or more of a subsidiary for-profit corporation, the parent organization must pay corporate income tax on the rents and interest that it receives from this controlled subsidiary.

There are two modifications of this rule. If some of the income of the subsidiary is derived from an activity that would be tax-exempt if it were carried on by the parent organization, then a proportionate share of the earnings distributed to the parent will

---

[2]It need not pay tax on rental income if substantially most (more than 85 percent) of the property is used for exempt purposes, *or* if the property is in the neighborhood of existing property being used for exempt purposes and will itself be used for exempt purposes within the next ten years (*Lawyer's Manual*, pp. 325–328). An accountant or tax lawyer should be consulted for the details on this issue.

be tax-exempt. Similarly, if the subsidiary itself is tax-exempt, all earnings which it distributes to the parent are tax-exempt, except for those earnings that are derived from an unrelated business activity.

In sum, it generally will not make any difference for tax purposes whether activities are carried on by the parent or the controlled subsidiary; tax liability is determined by the nature of the activity, not its organizational format. But if the parent organization owns *less* than 80 percent of the subsidiary, then the rent and interest received by the parent will always be tax-exempt. This is an important advantage of having less than 80 percent ownership in a subsidiary corporation.

Advantages of Other Degrees of Ownership (50 percent or less Ownership)

Create Maximum Options for Input. Minority ownership allows for the greatest equity participation and controlling voice by persons other than the parent organization. The parent may provide seed money to attract other investment to provide additional needed capital not otherwise available. An entrepreneur, employees, or the community may be the major shareholders.

For instance, the Kentucky Highlands CDC is generally the minority shareholder in its business ventures. Its purpose is to establish local businesses, and it sees benefits in giving up control to an entrepreneur, whose substantial capital investment in the business reinforces his or her commitment to making the venture successful. The entrepreneur must, in addition, be given authority to run the operation commensurate with that capital investment. Kentucky Highlands' control comes largely from the initial selections of the most promising entrepreneurs to take charge.

Avoid Stigma. As described before, a business may be stigmatized by too-close ties to a nonprofit, politically oriented, or social service program. Minority ownership may be a remedy.

THE INCUBATION PERIOD

Not all of the decisions about organizational structure need to be taken at once, and decisions about structure are not immutable. They may be changed to adapt to changed circumstances. In general, research undertaken by The University of Illinois at Chicago Center for Urban Economic Development found that a significant nurturing period is required to develop a revenue-generating venture.[3] During this period, questions about scale and complexity, the market, management, financing, and organizational structure need to be addressed. This requires planning, but also actual experience implementing the revenue-generating venture.

In the development process culminating in a for-profit operation, organizations will usually need to increase significantly the scale and complexity of their operations. For instance, the Jane Addams Center youth training program in Chicago, precursor to

[3]See Robert Mier and Wim Wiewel, "Business Activities of Not-for-Profit Organizations: Surviving the New Federalism?" *Journal of the American Planning Association*, August 1983: 316–325.

Spread The News, Inc., a mailing and distribution business operated by trainees, had an annual budget of approximately $50,000, only $2,500 of which was generated by sales of mailing and distribution services. Analysis showed that the minimum sales needed by a financially self-sufficient business was $150,000. In addition to obvious increases in scale, entirely new administrative functions such as marketing and management of accounts receivable were required. As the center grew, it had to constantly reconsider every aspect of the existing organization and its proposed business. Everything from the relationship to the constituency to employee qualifications and pay scales becomes an object of scrutiny.

Another reason for a nurturing period is the need to develop and hold a niche in the market. There may be a need for a product or service, but little initial actual demand. People may not be ready or able to spend money on, say, energy conservation products, important as they may be. Service and product development may take time to accomplish, and casting it out as a separate entity, if done hastily, will weaken its chance of success. In the Jane Addams case, the would-be entrepreneurs had to sort out where they were going to be positioned in a market that already existed and was reasonably competitive. This required a comparison of direct mailing versus door-to-door distribution services, and an evaluation of the relative advantages of serving one neighborhood vs. developing a citywide clientele.

A third reason why a nurturing period is needed is that it takes time to transform nonprofit management skills and value systems into a business-like approach. For instance, in the social services, a clientele can often be assumed and customers don't need to be actively recruited. Marketing, when performed, is sporadic and inexpert. In other nonprofit organizations, volunteer commitment sometimes makes up for financial or organizational shortfalls. In a business, however, especially one not run by an owner/entrepreneur, there appears to be less margin for error. While not-for-profit agencies frequently experience the same cash flow problems that businesses do, overall margins for error appear wider.

If new staff who already possess the needed business skills are hired, it will take time to integrate them sufficiently into the value system of the parent organization. For instance, one housing rehabilitation organization, which had started its own for-profit construction company, hired an experienced private contractor as manager. However, he felt that dealing with government subsidized housing rehabilitation, which the market study had identified as most promising, was too cumbersome. As a result the company sought to serve a private suburban market, thus defeating one of its purposes—providing reliable construction services in the neighborhood. To avoid such situations, it may well be worthwhile for an organization to invest in helping its own staff make the transition to business management. This may take time.

This issue of differing values between nonprofit organizations and businesses may recur in many different ways. In a 1984 survey of 26 nonprofit (mostly social service) organizations that operate business enterprises, Elizabeth Montgomery found that the two most frequently listed objectives were "job creation and training" and "income for programs and services."[4] She also presents the example of an arts organization, where the conflict occurs in a different way. The organization may have to choose between continuing a successful revival of a performance and pursuing the theater's stated purpose of producing new works. Those in charge of ticket sales may push for continuing the successful production, while the director and members of the cast for the next play take the opposite point of view. If the payroll depends on box-office revenues, every individual may feel the conflict personally.

However, the survey respondents also noted that some resolution and ranking of the priorities is essential and that over time business objectives tended to become more important. This is also reflected in personnel practices. Although several of the interviewed organizations were considering forms of worker ownership, most used standard business compensation and reward programs and sales incentives.

Throughout this entire nurturing period, technical assistance may often be helpful or even necessary. In many cases, planning and management assistance is required to sort things out and assist in the process of thinking through complex decisions. Technical aspects of the process include market and financial feasibility studies, organizational planning and the development of management systems, physical planning and design, and education about the nature and impact of the new ventures. Because the organizations starting the businesses are not solely driven by the profit motive, but rather by complex social and political motives, traditional business consulting has limited applicability. Often the organizations assemble teams of technical assistance providers from diverse sources such as their own boards, local law and accounting firms, financial institutions, and local universities.

How the cooperation between consultants and nonprofit organizations in this process gets structured reflects both the technical and organizational sophistication of the organization and its political direction. For a less sophisticated organization, a close, continuous relationship, where the consultants raise questions as much as they answer them, is appropriate. A sophisticated group may be able to ascertain its needs quite specifically and may be interested only in a short-term, traditional, client-consultant relationship. In either case, those who initiate business ventures must realize that their association with a parent nonprofit presents them with problems even greater than those faced by the ordinary small business person. Only extra effort in planning and thinking through all the issues will give them a chance at success.

[4]Elizabeth P. Montgomery, "Dual Objective Enterprises: Changing Attitudes and Values of Nonprofit Organizations Operating Business Ventures" (M.A. thesis, DePaul University, Chicago, 1984).

8

Retail Merchandising in Smaller Nonprofit Institutions

ELLIOTT N. LANG

RETAIL MERCHANDISING is a popular vehicle for generating earned income in nonprofit institutions. Most nonprofits sell something to the public but the majority make very little money from their efforts. This chapter presents some guidelines for determining an institution's retail merchandising potential and suggests a strategy for implementing a successful program. It focuses on small- and medium-sized nonprofit organizations—those with annual operating budgets of less than $2 million.

The typical nonprofit institution must build a retail merchandising program without the benefit of a spectacular circumstance. For example, small museums cannot attract blockbuster exhibitions or create licensing programs that use commercial channels of distribution. The income they generate will necessarily be modest—but potentially significant within the context of the operations of the institution. A successful retail marketing venture should generate gross sales of at least $50,000 annually.

SIZING UP THE MARKET

The success of any retail business depends on developing a market for specific goods and services. Nonprofits do not have the luxury of choosing their market; it is predetermined by the institution's mission, its programming and the audience it attracts.

An understanding of the institution's market is vital in determining whether a retail merchandising program is a viable option to generate earned income. Sample surveys should be used to develop a socio-economic profile of the audience and to determine the appeal of various types of merchandise. These surveys need not be elaborate or costly but they must produce accurate, usable data. Chart I provides an example of a survey that can be used by museums seeking to create or expand a retail business.

CHART I. Exit Survey of the Museum's Audience

Hi, my name is _____. I work for the Museum. We are conducting a survey that will help us to improve our services to the community. May I take just a few minutes of your time?

I. Why did you come to the Museum today?

    A. See the Exhibition.   (   )

    B. Use the bathroom.   (   )

    C. Curiosity.   (   )

    D. Other _____

_____
(Please describe)

II. How many times have you been in the Museum in the last twelve months?

    A. Once.   (   )

    B. Twice.   (   )

    C. Three times.   (   )

    D. More than three times. (   )

III. What did you particularly enjoy about the museum today?

_____

_____

_____

_____
(Please describe)

IV. What can we do to make your future visits more enjoyable?

_____

_____

_____
(Please describe)

V. Are you familiar with any of our educational programs for adults and children?

Yes (   )   No (   )

If yes, what programs do you know about?

_____

_____

_____

_____
(Please describe)

VI. What other Museums have you visited in the last twelve months?

_____

_____

_____

_____
(Please list)

VII. Are there other people with you today?
    A. Alone.   (   )
    B. Spouse.   (   )
    C. Friends.   (   )
    D. Children.   (   )
       How old are they? _____
    E. Other _____
                          (Please describe)

VIII. Are you married (   )   or   single (   )?

IX. Do you have children?   Yes (   )   No (   ).
    If yes, how old are they?

X. Where do you live?
    Town _____
    Zip Code _____

XI. How old are you?
    18–22   (   )   23–34   (   )
    35–44   (   )   45–54   (   )
    55–64   (   )   65 or Older (   )

XII. What is your occupation? _____

XIII. Sex of respondent: Male (   )   Female (   )

An institution's membership and annual attendance should total at least 50,000 adults and families. If the audience consists predominantly of school groups, attendance should total at least 100,000 annually. Such traffic can produce gross sales in the range of $50,000–$200,000 annually and a profit margin in excess of 20 percent of sales.

The demographics of the market are as important as its size. For example, an audience with a high level of education and disposable income is an asset to a fine arts museum or a center for the performing arts. A high socio-economic audience profile is less important in children's and science museums, or in zoos and botanical gardens, because they attract much larger numbers of people.

Institutions that charge admission or sell memberships can determine the size of their attendance easily. If the admission charge varies by visitor category, the institution also can determine the number of adults, senior citizens, and children in its audience. For institutions that offer several categories of membership (and most do), the number of people in each category will indicate whether the membership is oriented towards individuals or families.

Frequently, the results from the data collection are surprising to nonprofit administrators. They discover that the community they thought they were serving differs from their actual audience. Organizations also can analyze membership by zip code, using their mailing lists, to obtain additional socio-economic data. With the results of the survey (or surveys) in hand, the institution can begin to plan its retail merchandising program.

A study of the institution's audience has obvious benefits in developing programming and a membership campaign as well. It should be a priority for any nonprofit interested in growth.

ANALYZING THE COMPETITION

Part of the process in determining an institution's retail market involves an assessment of local competition. The task is important, not only to find out what competitors are doing but also to learn what they *aren't* doing. This could suggest important strategies in developing the retail venture. The most successful nonprofit retail merchandising programs are based on a merchandise assortment that is unique or has limited distribution within the institution's geographic area.

Senior staff members and perhaps members of the board of trustees should visit commercial and other nonprofit retail shops located in their metropolitan areas. For example, if a nonprofit is considering selling posters and prints, other retail print and framing shops should be visited. The observers should ask themselves what will make their shop better than the competition—the quality of the posters? The price? The service?

The fact that there may be a large number of competitors in the local area does not mean that another cannot succeed. Often several similar businesses clustered in one location indicate a market that already exists and need not be created from scratch. The most obvious example of a high concentration of nonprofit shops is in midtown Manhattan, especially along Fifth Avenue's "Museum Mile." Six institutions have retail shops and all are more or less successful. What these institutions know is that they must find a market niche for their visitors and members, and then fill it well.

On the other hand, there may be little competition. This can indicate an opportunity or a warning that the market is not interested in purchasing the merchandise. If you cannot find a McDonald's, people do not eat many hamburgers.

THE MERCHANDISE ASSORTMENT

The results of the market analysis and the comparison shopping should be viewed in relation to the institution's mission and its programming. This will determine the type of merchandise and the range of prices in the retail shop. In general, merchandise should relate to the institution's programs in order to appeal to its natural audience. The quality of the design and manufacture should be superior to the standards of local department stores. The merchandise must have an appeal that differentiates it from potential or actual competition.

The range of merchandise that can be sold is vast. It may include paper products such as postcards, note cards, calendars, posters and prints; books, records and tapes;

jewelry; scarves and neckties; items for the home; children's educational products; and souvenirs such as T-shirts and tote bags.

There are three potential sources for merchandise: the wholesale marketplace, crafts fairs and the institution's own product development efforts. Each source has advantages and disadvantages.

The wholesale marketplace offers a variety of products that may be related to the institution's programs and attractive to its market. However, quality merchandise often is difficult to find in commercial markets. The greater the distance from the source, the more costly it will be to shop for and acquire merchandise. Over time, good working relationships with wholesale vendors can be developed. The institution must constantly search the wholesale market for attractive new products to offer its members and visitors.

There are several guidelines regarding the pricing of this merchandise. The suggested retail price of commercial merchandise normally is double the cost, producing an initial markup of 50 percent of retail sales. The initial markup on books, records and tapes will be somewhat less, particularly if they are purchased in small quantities. Although these markups may appear attractive, they produce a profit margin of only 40 percent of sales as a result of other costs such as freight, markdowns on slow selling merchandise and inventory shrinkage. Obviously, tight control of operating expenses is crucial in generating significant levels of income from the sale of commercially produced products.

Handcrafted merchandise offers an opportunity for higher initial markups because the items are less likely to be sold in commercial retail outlets. Distinctive products help to differentiate the shop from the competition. On the other hand, it is difficult to build a retail merchandising program using handcrafted merchandise. Craftspeople often produce "one-of-a-kind" items, making bulk orders or repeat sales impossible. Since the product depends on hand labor, consistent, timely supply can be a problem. Smaller stores try to develop close working relationships with craftspeople in order to avoid these problems.

Products developed from an institution's collections or programming have the greatest appeal to its audience. Moreover, the institution can control distribution and obtain high profit margins from its own products. Unfortunately, small- and medium-sized nonprofits seldom have the financial resources to develop the number of products required to sustain an ongoing retail merchandising program.

Postcards, note cards, Christmas cards, posters, and calendars offer the greatest product development opportunities. The financial outlay for them need not be large and the rate of sale usually is high. These products have a broad appeal to visitors and members who want to leave the institution with a memento of their visit. Moreover, markups frequently are three to four times the initial cost. Other nonprofits may be interested in purchasing these items for resale as part of their own retail merchandising programs, creating a wholesale business for the institutions that originated the products.

The selection of merchandise is the most important factor in developing a successful retail merchandising program. The merchandise mix should be based on a carefully designed and edited selection of goods purchased from both commercial wholesalers and craftspeople. Product development should be limited to merchandise that requires a minimal investment in relation to potential sales. The actual selection of merchandise requires a detailed understanding of the institution's audience.

THE MARKETING VEHICLE—A CATALOG OR A RETAIL SHOP?

A common question asked by nonprofit institutions is: Should we produce a mail order catalog? In most cases, the answer is no! Few nonprofit institutions have the expertise or the financial resources required for direct-mail marketing beyond a membership campaign. Moreover, the mail order catalog business is notoriously risky and extremely competitive.

The economics of direct-mail marketing make the risks readily apparent. The rate of response to a catalog mailing seldom exceeds 2.5 percent. An institution that mails 400,000 catalogs cannot expect to generate more than 10,000 mail orders. Assuming the average size order is for $35, the mailing would produce $350,000 in sales.

The cost of the mailing, however, is as follows:

Preparation of copy, photography, layout, printing, and mailing 400,000 catalogs @ 50¢ each	$200,000
Rental of 400,000 names @ $50 per thousand	20,000
Order fulfillment (contracted out)	25,000
Merchandise (50 percent of gross sales)	175,000
Total	$420,000

The enterprise would produce a loss of $70,000 on sales of $350,000.

A retail shop offers a far more practical option for small- and medium-sized institutions. In contrast to the mail order catalog business the economics of a shop make sense.

A retail shop in a nonprofit institution benefits from certain efficiencies and subsidies provided by the parent. The enterprise usually enjoys rent-free space and is provided with heat, light, and power. Commercial retail businesses pay between 10 and 15 percent of sales for these occupancy costs. Payroll expenses often are lower because volunteers frequently provide a majority of the workforce. Even when the staff is paid, salaries usually are at the federal minimum wage level. As a result of low operating costs, successful nonprofit retail shops can generate a profit margin of more than 20 percent of sales.

The retail shop should not be smaller than 300 square feet in order to provide enough space to offer a reasonable merchandise selection. Most nonprofit shops are 300–750 square feet in size.

It may cost $50 to $75 per square foot to design and create the shop. Merchandise should be presented to its best advantage. Fixtures and lighting should highlight the merchandise and create an ambience that reflects the character of the institution.

Customers should be encouraged to handle merchandise. Reserve stock should be housed in the selling fixtures to facilitate customer service and control payroll expense. Needless to say, the selection of an architect or designer for the shop is a critical decision.

The shop should be located at the entrance to the institution. Shops located in out-of-the-way places invariably fail. As a result, the shop will be the visitor's first and last impression of the institution.

PROJECTING SALES

A shop cannot operate successfully without a business plan. Sales projections are the most important part of the plan. Commercial retailers know that "volume hides all their sins." When sales are good, profits are high. When sales are poor, profits disappear quickly, despite efforts to control inventory and operating expenses.

Actual gross sales are the result of two factors: the number of sales transactions and the average dollar amount of each purchase. The number of transactions depends on the institution's attendance and the percentage of people who purchase. The sales projection should be updated at least once a month based on actual results.

Gross profit depends on the average markup of the merchandise purchased, freight cost, markdowns and inventory shrinkage.

Operating expenses obviously must be included in the income projection. They may include such costs as payroll and fringe benefits, supplies, telephone, credit card commissions, cash shortages, interest expense, etc.

The business plan will determine both the break-even point and the potential to generate income. If the sales required to break even are beyond the reach of the institution, it should seek other ways to generate income. If the potential income is insignificant in terms of the institution's annual operating budget, more fruitful possibilities for income generation should be explored.

The most critical financial requirement in retailing is producing an adequate cash flow. Without it, the business cannot operate from day to day.

The supermarket business is a classic illustration of retail cash flow. The average supermarket generates a profit of less than 2 percent of sales. The money invested in fixtures and inventory could yield a guaranteed return of more than 10 percent in a secure financial instrument without the headaches of running a business. However, the supermarket's return on invested capital can be close to 20 percent because its merchandise turns over many times in a single week. As a result, a good supermarket generates a cash flow that exceeds the operating requirements of its business. The money can be used for other purposes including building new stores and investing in other businesses.

Retailers generate cash flow by controlling both their operating expenses and the size of their inventory.

The shop should have a budget to purchase merchandise that is adjusted every month based on actual sales results. The shop manager should maintain a log of outstanding purchase orders and merchandise receipts that can be compared to the budget. Retailers refer to this comparison as their *open-to-buy*.

Markdowns should be taken periodically to dispose of slow-selling merchandise and to create capital that can be invested in fresh inventory. Every retailer makes mistakes in selecting merchandise. Good retailers take markdowns to correct their mistakes; poor ones allow their money to be tied up in dead inventory.

It should be obvious that a retail merchandising program offers potential benefits beyond the generation of income. The program can be important in promoting the educational mission and the general financial health of the institution. For example, museums or art centers usually offer members or subscribers a discount on merchandise purchases. Often, the discount on merchandise can produce savings greater than the cost of a membership or subscription. This can be a tangible incentive to support the institution.

Despite these additional benefits, a retail merchandising program must justify its existence on the basis of income, cash flow and return on invested capital. Ventures that operate at a loss simply do not make sense in the nonprofit world.

FINANCING THE VENTURE

Retailing is a capital-intensive business. It requires funds for store construction and the initial inventory as well as a cash reserve to cover expenses until the business begins to produce a cash flow. The total initial investment can easily exceed $50,000.

Few nonprofits can finance a retail merchandising program from their operating budgets. Funding may require assistance from board members, foundations, or government agencies.

A group of trustees may be willing to donate money or lend it to the institution at little or no cost. Or they may make a challenge grant to the organization or provide a loan guarantee. These contributions, loans, or guarantees should represent an additional trustee commitment. Otherwise, primary institutional activities will suffer from the movement of funds into the retail program.

Financial assistance may be available from private foundations and public corporations interested in developing earned income opportunities in nonprofit organizations. In the New York area, the Robert Sterling Clark Foundation, the J. M. Kaplan Fund, Inc., The New York Community Trust, and the Exxon Corporation have provided funds to develop retail programs in nonprofit institutions.

At the federal government level, the National Endowment for the Arts, the National Endowment for the Humanities, and the Institute of Museum Services have provided financial assistance. City and state agencies with similar goals have provided support as well.

Government agencies, private corporations, and foundations share common concerns. They want to make certain that nonprofit retail merchandising programs have been well conceived and have a good chance for success. They will require a marketing and business plan and expect the institution to demonstrate its confidence in the project by sharing in the financial risk.

SOME OPERATIONAL CONSIDERATIONS

A retail merchandising program is an anomaly in a nonprofit environment. Nonprofit institutions exist to educate, to provide cultural experiences, to serve the community, or to collect and preserve for the future.

Often, choices must be made between these goals and the institution's commercial interests. For example, the retail shop may need additional selling space but its expansion may involve reducing the space available for exhibitions. A shop may carry books that seldom sell but are necessary to project and enhance the educational mission of the organization. Sales growth may require an additional investment in inventory that is unaffordable because the money is required for other purposes.

The person at the center of the retail merchandising program is the shop manager. The ability and interest of this person is a critical factor in the success of the institution's retail merchandising program.

The shop manager may or may not be paid. Sometimes he or she is a volunteer, working in concert with other volunteers who comprise the backbone of the sales force. The manager may face the unusual management task of integrating paid and unpaid labor. In addition, he or she usually serves as the buyer, the stockperson, the clerical support, and the principal salesperson. The manager may also take the daily receipts to the bank and audit the cash register tapes.

As a result of these multiple demands, many important retailing functions often take a back seat to immediate operating needs. For example, planning and controlling inventory levels and the work required to find and develop merchandise, may become low-priority activities.

The turnover of shop managers in nonprofit institutions is high. The pressures are great and the career opportunities are limited. The manager seldom has the educational background or experience to qualify for advancement to curatorial, artistic, or administrative positions in the institution. The lack of a career path and low salaries make it difficult for small- and medium-sized nonprofits to attract people with commercial retail experience.

To ameliorate these factors, shop managers must get organizational and financial support from the director of the institution. Managers should be brought into discussions that affect their work and serve on relevant committees. They should be treated as "first-class" citizens by other members of the institution's staff.

A trustee committee can also assist the shop manager. Trustees will be interested in monitoring the retail merchandising program because of its visibility, its impact on the operating budget, and its investment in inventory. Committees, hopefully with some professional retail or financial experience, can provide guidance and even hands-on help.

Finally, the accounting and systems requirements for a retail enterprise are totally different from those in other areas of the institution. Procedures must be established to control inventory and track outstanding purchase orders. Sales and inventory must be reported by category of merchandise. Markdowns must be recorded. Cash must be controlled. The institution's business will experience an increase in workload that may require an increase in staff.

POTENTIAL TAX LIABILITIES

A few words should be said regarding the tax considerations in a nonprofit retail venture. The Internal Revenue Code states that for activities of nonprofit organizations to be exempt from tax, they must be "substantially related" to the exempt mission of the organization. This includes merchandise sold in gift shops. In recent years, the Internal Revenue Service has audited retail shops in nonprofit institutions and, in certain cases, has assessed these institutions for taxes due on the sale of unrelated merchandise. Indeed, IRS agents have applied the *fragmentation rule* in their activities. Under this rule, each item for sale in the retail shop may be individually reviewed for its relationship to the exempt mission of the organization. Those not deemed substantially related may be taxed.

The activities of the IRS have created a number of misconceptions regarding tax liability and have led to the false impression that the institution's nonprofit status could be in jeopardy if it strays too far from its mission.

In reality, the potential tax liability is limited. Few of the smaller nonprofit retail shops actually have been audited and, of those that were, only a small percentage have been found to sell unrelated merchandise. The items themselves normally represent a small part of the total merchandise assortment—usually a few jewelry, gift, or miscellaneous items. Books, posters, prints, paper products, and children's educational merchandise are seldom questioned. To date, a potential problem has not become a major practical concern.

There are measures that an institution can take to protect itself and its shop from a difficult audit. First, it is most important to comply with the spirit of the law. Since merchandise related to the institution is more likely to sell in the shop than merchandise generally available in commercial retail establishments, the Tax Code actually offers a sound merchandising principle for store managers.

Second, the shop can demonstrate the educational value of its merchandise. For example, a small card placed next to each item in a display case can present information that relates the merchandise to the institution's collections, exhibitions, and educational programs. This is an effective selling tool as well.

Third, the retail accounting system should reflect both the direct and indirect costs of operating the retail shop in order to correctly state the income generated by the enterprise. The IRS permits institutions to charge their shops for legitimate business expenses. An auditor will be less likely to raise questions if the shop's income is correctly and clearly derived as well as reasonable in comparison with the institution's total operating budget. Indeed, the only risk is that some tax may be due on a portion of the income—dollars that would not have existed at all without the retail program.

A CASE STUDY

Building a profitable retail business is not as straightforward as applying the principles and guidelines in this chapter. There are often false starts and troublesome problems. The following case study illustrates the growth of a typical nonprofit retail enterprise. The institution is a medium-sized fine arts museum with an annual attendance of 100,000, which includes 30,000 children in school groups. The museum has 7,000 members and an annual budget of $1,000,000.

The museum's retail shop generated sales of $35,000 annually. It was operating at a loss. The shop occupied 475 square feet of space in a corner of the main floor and was not visible to visitors from the entrance to the museum. It had a staff of four including a paid manager and part-time employees and volunteers.

The shop's merchandise consisted of items that did not relate to the museum's collections, exhibitions, or public programming. It was an unfocused mix of lucite boxes, coloring books, yarn, place mats, T-shirts, maps, kites, etc. Much of the inventory was more than a year old.

Marketing data indicated that the institution was in a high-growth metropolitan area whose population would grow by 20 percent to 600,000 within three years. More significantly, the socio-economic profile of the population was typical of an audience interested in fine arts museums. Approximately 30 percent of the population consisted of professionals, managers, and business officials.

Based on the size and character of the museum's actual and potential audience, the trustees were willing to consider a major investment to develop a new 1,000-square-foot shop at the entrance to the institution. They engaged a consultant to help plan the enterprise.

As part of the consultant's field work, visits were made to other stores in the area. These visits indicated that a merchandise assortment could be developed that would be unique in the museum's marketplace. There was an opportunity to establish a quality fine arts oriented retail business and a large customer base to support it.

The consultant suggested a merchandise assortment that included art books, prints, posters, paper products, jewelry, gifts, and children's educational products. Prints, posters, and paper products would be purchased from other fine arts institutions. Jewelry, gifts, and children's items would be obtained from small commercial suppliers with limited distribution among retail stores in the metropolitan area. The consultant would work with the museum to develop its own postcards, note cards, Christmas cards, and a desk calendar, using images from its collections.

Three projections of sales and income were prepared based on various levels of museum attendance, the average sale in each merchandise category, the cost of merchandise, and operating expenses. The program's goal was to generate $250,000 in sales and $50,000 in net income annually in three to four years. Projections indicated that the shop would cover its own cash needs after the first three months of operation.

An investment of $125,000 was required to implement the program: $70,000 to design and build the new shop, $35,000 for merchandise, and $20,000 for a contingency fund to cover initial operating expenses.

The merchandising program was approved by the director of the museum and its board of trustees. A group of trustees provided a five-year loan without interest to fund the program. Work began on store design and construction, merchandise orders were placed with suppliers, products were designed and produced, and systems were installed to control inventory. The staff was expanded to a total of twelve full-time and part-time people. The new shop took nine months to plan and build. It opened on schedule.

Sales in the first three months were 35 percent below projections. As a result, the cash reserve was in danger of depletion and the museum faced the possibility of borrowing more money to cover the shop's operating expenses.

An analysis of sales and inventory was undertaken. It indicated that a number of items, principally at the $30 and above price range (at retail), had not sold. There was price resistance to expensive art books, posters, and gifts. Sales of paper goods, children's merchandise, and jewelry were much stronger than expected. The customer response to the merchandise assortment indicated that there were opportunities to turn the business around.

Immediately, a number of expensive art books were returned to publishers for credit. Markdowns were taken on slow-moving merchandise to obtain the cash to buy more paper goods, jewelry, children's merchandise, and less expensive art books. Displays were changed to feature the new items. The results were dramatic. Sales in the following two months were within 5 percent of the original plan and the cash flow provided funds for other museum activities.

Three years later, the shop's annual sales are slightly above $200,000. Income is close to $40,000. Loan repayments to the trustees are on schedule. The business will achieve its financial objectives, but it will take a year longer than projected to achieve them.

The shop has made a major contribution to the ambience of the museum and has enhanced its reputation in the community. Membership has grown to 23,000 and annual attendance has increased by almost 50 percent. The museum shop helped to produce these results.

This illustration exemplifies the opportunities and pitfalls in creating a retail merchandising program as well as the problems inherent in starting a new business venture. Good planning was just the beginning. The museum also had to make a major commitment to develop the business, adjust its operations based on actual performance, and stick with it long enough to achieve its original financial objectives. The results have been rewarding but they were not easy to accomplish.

The standards applied in planning and executing the retail venture cannot be compromised. If the nonprofit is not prepared to do it the right way, it should not do it at all.

9

Stepping Out into the Marketplace: The Pitfalls of Earned Income for the Small Nonprofit

NANCY E. HAYCOCK

THE ISSUE OF EARNED INCOME typically surfaces for the small nonprofit in two ways. The first is through financial pressure. Fund raising isn't going very well, or a government contract has been cut in half, or the organization is running out of money. Someone then proposes charging a fee for service or selling something as the best way to survive. The second entry point is through the identification of a gap in service. The private sector isn't providing it, so the nonprofit decides to see if it can perform the service at a "reasonable cost." Both approaches to earned income are fraught with danger.

Small nonprofit organizations are, by definition, groups with little or no endowment, few formal long-range plans, and generally informal personnel practices. Typically, their operating budgets include very little administrative money, although they may have millions of dollars in program contracts. The staff is commonly overworked, and many serve only in a part-time capacity. They are fighting some impossible cause like hunger or homelessness, and they are underpaid and overworked.

Nearly all small nonprofits must deal with certain basic issues in order to create a successful earned income venture. The first is time. The director and staff are already stretched thin. There are contracts and grants to be complied with, staff to be supervised, an important service to render to a needy community, and a board of directors that demands care and feeding. It is very difficult to find the time to devote to an earned income venture. Second, there is no way to earn a significant amount of money quickly. If an organization is in a severe cash squeeze, chances are poor that rescue will come from selling T-shirts or running a thrift shop. Third, small nonprofits have little leeway in the use of available funds, a problem that can lead to undercapitalization. Fourth, most small nonprofits do not have a realistic notion of what their internal costs are, and when they try to project the costs of their earned income venture, they have a lot of trouble. Often their estimates are too low. In many cases, they don't include overhead, or the value of their own time.

Finally, few small nonprofits have a realistic understanding of the marketplace. They still view themselves as outside the market economy, and frequently equate need for service with a market. For example, just because a senior center needs to buy vegetables doesn't mean that it will buy from a local nonprofit organization, even if it does have cheaper prices and nicer salespeople. Many factors go into a person's decision to buy.

The following ten case studies illustrate the kinds of conditions and situations that small nonprofit organizations confront as they venture for the first time into the area of earned income and enterprise. They are actual case histories drawn from the work of Community Resource Exchange, a management consulting group based in New York City. The names of the groups have been changed.

CALL FOR FOOD

T-Shirt Sales

Call for Food is a citywide information and referral center that works directly with emergency food providers and with those in need of emergency food. It began to explore the idea of earned income when its funding fell to half what it had been the previous year. The motivation was purely financial. Call for Food had no income to spare and only one full-time staff person. Its project is a good example of a first effort for a small nonprofit.

Call for Food approached a radio station—KISS-FM—and asked it to sponsor the sale of some item that would have the radio station's name on it, with all proceeds of that item to go toward general support of Call for Food. This sort of endorsement is frequently done by radio stations. KISS-FM agreed to advertise T-shirts, for which they would charge $8.50. The contractual arrangement was that KISS-FM would pay the total cost of the T-shirts and advertise them, along with a public service announcement for Call for Food, for a period of six weeks. Orders would be sent to the radio station and then forwarded to Call for Food, where they would then be recorded and mailed.

After two months, Call for Food had orders from 1,000 people, which netted $5,000 after mailing costs—for them, a very significant amount. However, this profit did not factor in the cost of a bookkeeper or the volunteers who did all the mailings. If Call for Food had had to pay for the T-shirts or any of this staff time, the total income would have been much less.

This sort of venture is hard to make profitable unless there are some in-kind contributions. It is, however, a good learning step for groups who may be considering a more serious earned income venture for the future. It is also one of the most common ways that small nonprofits supplement their government contracts and foundation grants.

CLARK HENRY DEVELOPMENT COMPANY

Calendar Sales

Clark Henry Development Company is a neighborhood improvement organization that was established in 1977 to preserve and upgrade housing and commercial streets in a section of South Brooklyn. Clark Henry provides information to tenants, works with merchants and city agencies to improve the appearance of the area, and promotes the neighborhood through street fairs and other special events. It is primarily funded by one state housing agency, the Division of Housing and Community Renewal. This funding is supplemented by small grants from banks and grassroots fund-raising events. As a neighborhood preservation company, Clark Henry has little opportunity to raise significant foundation dollars. Unless it can fund raise around some special onetime project, it must rely on individual support to leverage its budget. None of its fund-raising efforts have raised more than $500 or $600, and generally the work involved has been extensive.

This past year, the board of directors decided to try to raise substantially more money involving less volunteer and staff time. It came up with the idea of a calendar of photographs of historic buildings in the agency's area. The board felt it could sell at least 1,500 calendars, at a price of $5 each. However, it ran into a lot of unforeseen costs. First, Clark Henry arranged to pay an artist $1,500 to do the layout and design of the calendar. As it turned out, this was an excessive expense. The photographs had been selected by a board member, and a simple graphic design would have been sufficient. The second mistake was in timing: The calendar was not printed until November. By that time, most stores were stocked with calendars. Nobody in the organization knew that September was the most common time for bulk calendar sales. As a result, sales were at a reduced level.

In the end, the cost to print the calendar was $3,200, and sales amounted to only $3,500. However, Clark Henry has decided to redo the calendar for the next year using the same layout and design. This would substantially reduce the cost of production. The organization believes it can make a profit of $2,000 the second time around.

CLEARINGHOUSE FOR THE INSTITUTIONALIZED AGED

Publication

The Clearinghouse is a self-help organization that was started in the mid-seventies to help friends and relatives of nursing home residents monitor the quality of care being provided in New York City. It has become recognized as a major advocate for the elderly. It runs a service for people looking for advice on placing elderly family members in homes, and for resolving complaints relating to inferior care. The Clearinghouse's staff and board are also active as advocates of institutional change in the quality of care available to nursing home consumers.

In the early years, the Clearinghouse's funding was entirely based upon foundation grants, which were not difficult to get in the 1970s when nursing home scandals kept the issue in the spotlight. In the 1980s, funding began to dry up, and the Clearinghouse had a harder time getting the attention of funders. This soon led to predictable cash flow crises.

At roughly the same time, the Clearinghouse decided to assemble a guide that would provide all the information a person in New York City would need to arrange for nursing home care. The Clearinghouse had seen its requests escalate while it was aware that no such guide was available. The organization raised foundation money to pay for the cost of producing the guide because it wanted to give it away free. However, because there was no staff money allocated in the budget, the manual took several years to complete, and by the time it was ready for printing, there was no money left from its grants. This forced the Clearinghouse to sell the guide. Hence, the Clearinghouse backed into what became an income-generating opportunity.

The Clearinghouse decided to tie the cost of its publication to a $15 membership fee. The only costs that it included when calculating expected income were a printing cost of $2.50 per copy and a postage cost of $1.60. Grant money was used to hire a publicist to place public service announcements and newspaper articles. The organization figured that its profit would be $11.90 per copy.

The guide received excellent coverage on radio stations and in all the major newspapers, including the *New York Times* and *New York* magazine. However, the difficulty in evaluating the success of sales is that copies were tied to membership. Since no membership drive was conducted in the two years after the guide was published, the growth in membership fees was probably a fairly good indicator of the guide's draw. In 1981, the Clearinghouse generated $3,500 in membership contributions. In 1982, the year the guide was published, membership sales soared to $18,000; in 1983, they increased to $25,000. Since the Clearinghouse's total budget was $100,000, this represented 25 percent of its operating income.

In 1985, the Clearinghouse decided to expand the guide for a statewide market. It has discovered that there is nothing comparable to their guide for New York City. This time, however, the organization will not have the same learning curve since the state guide will follow the same research and presentation format as the city guide. The Clearinghouse will not tie sales to membership this time, but instead will charge $25 and call that fee a contribution to the organization. This is in line with the board's strategy to increase its direct mail funding base.

KIDS CARE

Thrift Shop

Kids Care offers a variety of family support services to parents and child care providers on the Lower East Side of Manhattan. The organization has a large space where parents come to share information, and where children can use their toys and books. Kids Care also provides in-depth counseling about the type of child care that is most appropriate for an individual child, and offers training and support services for family day care providers.

Kids Care's annual operating budget is $50,000. It has never had an easy time raising that amount from foundations, and it has had to supplement its few grants with rummage sales, raffles, and other traditional grassroots fundraising. When the organization moved into larger quarters in 1983, the codirectors brainstormed about new ways to earn some revenue, and came up with the idea of a thrift shop for infants and children, where they would sell children's clothing, toys, and furniture.

The shop was planned to be run exclusively with volunteers, in a storage room which was repainted and redecorated. Flyers were printed and sent to all parents who had ever used Kids Care services, and posted in the shops of many local retailers.

After eighteen months, the results were mediocre—even though plenty of clothes, car seats, and toys have been donated by people in the neighborhood. In fact, there were too many donations for the volunteers to handle. Also, thrift shop hours were determined by the schedule of the volunteers, and this did not turn out to meet the demand. One of the codirectors wound up handling many sales and bookkeeping chores, spending about an hour a day on thrift shop business. This might have been cost effective if the shop had brought in a significant amount of money, but its sales never exceeded $200 a month.

The views of the staff about the success of the venture were telling. They felt the idea was a good one; indeed, without the thrift shop, Kids Care would have fallen behind on rental payments. The staff also believed that the thrift shop sometimes brought people to the center who otherwise would not have known about its services. In that way, it was functioning as a type of outreach.

Outreach, however, was not the primary purpose of the shop. On the other hand, it was doubtful the thrift shop could improve sales without changing its mode of operating. Its location within the offices of the center—on the third floor—meant that access was limited. Staff time to devote to the store was also limited. Volunteers were dedicated but erratic. Marketing was nonexistent. Kids Care has immediate survival needs and it is unlikely that a thrift shop, given such a low priority by the organization, will ever be able to make more than a small dent in the overall operating needs of the agency.

EQUAL EMPLOYMENT FOR WOMEN

Fee-For-Service

Equal Employment for Women was set up in 1975 as a research, training, and consultation center to advise working women on sexual harassment and gender-bias issues. It was one of the first organizations to tackle these problems. In its early years, it attacked the issue of sexual harassment mainly through direct service to women who had experienced harassment on the job. This was done through answering information requests and through telephone counseling with women in the New York City area. Over the years, this focus shifted as more groups began to offer counseling on the issue, and EEW began to concentrate its efforts on training seminars, lectures, and policy consultation with managers and administrators of government and private companies. By 1983, it had spun off most of its direct service components to other organizations, although it continued to do some training for these organizations.

This shift in focus was fiscally dictated. In its first six years, EEW had been funded by foundations, during a period when funders viewed the issue as "upcoming." By 1982, however, funders felt the issue had receded, and EEW's funding dried up. This provoked a major debate between board and staff members. They went through a great deal of soul searching in an effort to come to grips with the changed situation. The result was a year without funding, followed by a restructuring, and a renewed commitment to provide the service through fee-for-service arrangements.

The fiscal crisis made EEW reevaluate the value of its skills and experience, within the context of a marketplace. As the present director said:

> We used to give our service away. Now we began to look closely at who could honestly afford to pay us a fee. We had always had a sliding scale, but we had never taken it very seriously, and we didn't charge what it cost us to operate. I don't think we knew what it cost. We did know that the budgets of other nonprofits were shrinking, so we didn't think there was much of a potential market there. We sure didn't start out wanting to work with the profit sector, but we gradually came to realize that women workers were women workers, wherever they were. There was important work for us to do which was consistent with our mission of contributing to institutional change. All of this helped us to change.

Equal Employment for Women decided that it would not only stay in business, but it would also raise enough money through corporate contracts and consulting fees so it could continue its community work. Its market assessment indicated that it had a product that could be sold. Although there were other consultants doing this work, the others didn't have the same base of experience. EEW developed a sliding scale that ranged from $25–$50 an hour for a nonprofit organization to $125 an hour for a corporation, with variable arrangements for workshops and speeches.

EEW was able to get its price. The staff did have to make radical changes in their work style, however, including new clothes, new language, and a new habit of thinking about the value of time. Although far from flush after two years, EEW has managed to raise most of its budget through a combination of government contracts and several large, corporate contracts.

This is primarily a successful story of an organization that managed to get past a severe funding crisis, restructure, and provide services on a fee-for-service arrangement. In its first year, EEW spent 15 percent of its time with groups that could pay no fees. It was able to do this because its corporate contracts were paying at a rate somewhat above actual operating costs. Part of its ability to do this was its low overhead. Indeed, that was its competitive edge: Through all the changes, they held onto a small basement space, which cost only $200 a month, and kept staff salaries well below market. Now in its third year, EEW is hoping to attract a few foundation grants to pay for their free work. If able to do this, EEW will raise staff salaries and add a few amenities.

PROJECT OPEN DOOR

Corporate Membership

Project Open Door was set up in 1964 to assist people in securing their rights to the housing of their choice through use of the Fair Housing Laws, and to bring class action suits to attack discrimination on a broad scale.

At first, the organization was largely supported by federal antipoverty grants, but when that program was reorganized, the antidiscrimination activities no longer fit the new guidelines. The director decided to save the service by separately incorporating—and partially supporting—the organization's work by providing relocation and counseling services to major New York City companies. Since Project Open Door had already compiled a lot of this housing information as part of its discrimination service, the director felt this would not entail much extra work.

Project Open Door began by researching which headquarters offices of U.S. companies were located in New York City, and then sent letters to the presidents of hundreds of those companies. It took a year to bring in the first corporate contract. During this time, however, costs were minimized. Only one staff person, the previous director, was on staff, and space costs were donated.

Success came slowly. Part of the slowness could be attributed to the fact that Project Open Door was offering a service that hadn't existed before. Although real estate brokers were plentiful, no one combined listings with counseling like Project Open Door now offered. However, employee benefits were an area of growth for many companies and, over time, the idea of a housing placement service as a fringe benefit took hold. A foundation grant provided the cushion in the interim, and once the first corporation signed a contract, other companies followed suit.

Project Open Door developed several types of contracts. One was based on an annual retainer fee, with an additional charge for each employee referred. Another was a flat fee based on the total number of employees. When asked how she arrived at these figures, the director threw up her hands and said:

> I never knew how many employees would be referred or how much trouble they would be. I couldn't have figured out an hourly billable rate because we didn't keep those kinds of time records. But I knew that we typically spent about $500 helping someone find an apartment, and I took a shot in the dark and came up with $2 per employee per year. It was all rather guess work.

This guesswork happened to be quite good, and the service was so successful that by the end of two years, Project Open Door was receiving twice as much income from corporate contracts as from foundations.

In the second year, a new board member reviewed the income figures, and decided that because so much of its work was now going to its corporate relocation program, the organization might be jeopardizing its nonprofit tax status. This scrutiny started a process that led to a decision to establish a separate for-profit subsidiary for the corporate service.

In the organization's first year of operating separately, the corporate retainers amounted to $165,000, representing 35 different companies. The nonprofit center's income that same year was $75,000. The two corporations continued to share office space and supplies; half the director's salary was paid by the for-profit subsidiary, as well as some of the support costs.

Currently, the for-profit subsidiary is carrying many of the expenses of the nonprofit center. This is an important contribution because these operating costs are difficult to raise from foundations. Interestingly, the subsidiary has made it easier to raise money because funders are enthusiastic about successful business ventures. To be sure, the subsidiary would never be able to support more than a percentage of the nonprofit center's costs. As the director stated, "It's important that funders aren't let off the hook. They should be supporting the services of the center for those who don't come under any corporate contract." The partial subsidy of the center gives it a flexibility that it wouldn't otherwise have.

It is also important to note that this survival strategy took Project Open Door away from its original mission. It is spending a great deal of time providing a placement service for affluent businessmen and women. The founders never intended to set up an organization for that purpose. However, the center has remained open to work with at least some people who have experienced discrimination in their search for housing in New York, and it appears that without the corporate placement service, even these few would have had nowhere to go.

CHILDREN'S ADVOCATE

Corporate Membership

Children's Advocate is New York City's largest information service for parents seeking child care and early childhood programs. It also addresses the full range of child care issues relating to publicly and privately funded programs, and provides various technical services to child care programs. It was formed three years ago through the merger of two well known social service organizations.

One of the first priorities of the newly merged organization was to diversify its funding base, since both organizations had been extremely dependent on foundation funding. It arrived at a four-part approach to expand funding sources, which included corporations, government contracts, membership subscriptions, fundraising projects, and special events. It sought a foundation grant to hire a person to do corporate outreach to see if there was enough interest in providing child care services to employees. The organization obtained a three-year grant that led to a corporate membership program. Within two years, the program had grown to seventeen members, which amounted to $100,000 in contracts. The total operating budget at that point was $350,000.

Children's Advocate's corporate membership service was confined to telephone counseling on all forms of child care, and detailed information on individual centers. The service enhanced its overall program because it pushed the organization to solidify its relationship with all the resource and referral programs in the area. In addition, Children's Advocate viewed the corporate membership program as a "foot in the door," which allowed it to work closely with corporate management in the hope that the corporation would continue to expand their employee day care benefit. Interestingly, the organization did not think of the corporate membership service as a business, but rather as part of an overall effort to tap new funding resources for the organization.

Deciding on a membership fee was not easy. It was roughly based on prior experience with individuals. An average cost of placement was set at $50. (Research was done about how many employees would have children, and an estimate was made that 5 percent of them would call.) Only one type of membership was offered and that was based upon the number of employees. Corporations understood the fee concept and had no problem with the size of the charge. Still, it took nearly two years, on average, from the time of an initial conversation to the final, signed contract.

The director of the program felt that it was not necessary to have fancy or detailed materials to market the service. Children's Advocate used only a one-page flyer. Apparently, the total packaging of the "sale" was decisive, and the presence of a professional staff person counted for a great deal.

The crucial element of success in Children's Advocate's effort was that its service was an integral part of the organization. This meant there was no expensive learning period before the business could take off. It was also a service that satisfied a long-term political goal of the organization to educate employers to the need for child care services.

With all its success, Children's Advocate still does not know exactly what it is earning from the corporate membership program. When the project director was asked what the program earned this year, she said, "I *hope* we're making money. I'm not sure if we're doing better than breaking even." She noted that in the next year, more attention would be spent on developing actual hourly costs of running the program.

HOUSING DEVELOPMENT COUNCIL

Fuel Consortium

The Housing Development Council is a twelve-year-old New York City membership organization serving as a forum for the exchange of information and providing technical and other assistance for community-based housing groups. It was also designed as a vehicle to formulate and seek implementation for housing programs and policies that would better meet the needs of low- and moderate-income people. Priorities have shifted over the years according to the needs of members, but HDC remains the strongest housing advocate organization in the city.

In 1978, HDC started a fuel-buying consortium to help low-income housing projects in the city cope with the rising costs of fuel. The idea was to reduce the operating costs of these projects. There was no expectation on the part of the board or staff that there would be any earned income payoff. In fact, any money earned was to be passed on to consortium members, after it was clear that all expenses for the winter season had been paid. Grants were obtained to start the project, and federally funded CETA workers were used to run it. The council set a policy that all payments by members had to be made in advance of delivery.

The fuel business grew slowly. Moreover, from the first winter, it was discovered that prompt payment was unrealistic. The Housing Development Council soon found itself in a vulnerable position, having advanced thousands of dollars to the fuel company because certain buildings neglected to pay their bills. This was particularly problematic because HDC didn't know what its fuel-purchasing venture really cost to operate. No overhead costs had been allocated and bookkeeping was unsophisticated. As the director said, "It's mind-boggling, but true. We just didn't talk about the costs." Since the motive for starting the venture had been to provide a service, there were no management incentives, such as staff bonuses, built in. Indeed, as a whole, the staff was more interested in its advocacy work.

Two factors changed this picture. First, HDC began to be pressured by its funders to develop a self-sufficiency plan. Second, its accounts receivable grew to $127,000, or 40 percent of its operating budget. It was impossible to continue to ignore the fuel business. However, despite this drain, it also appeared that the fuel business was actually raising a considerable amount of money for HDC.

These pressures created a great deal of tension within the organization. Suddenly the fuel business appeared as an element of HDC's fund-raising strategy—one that it had to exploit in order to maintain its housing advocacy work. This forced a complete reexamination of the venture.

As a result of this assessment, the fuel-buying overhead was separated out from the rest of the organization's expenses. It began to be viewed as a straight business venture, the purpose of which was to make money for the advocacy work. The executive director and board envisioned a long-range goal of 50 percent of the operating costs of the organization being supported by the fuel business. In order to move toward that goal, new staff were hired who had business and marketing expertise. A consultant was also selected to figure out how to expand the base of customers from tenants of low-income buildings. The new plan was to stop recruiting these buildings and concentrate on homeowners in New Jersey and the Long Island area. Finance charges were also instituted on all accounts not paid after 30 days. Finally, a commission system for compensating the staff of the fuel business was implemented.

The restructuring paid off. This past year, the fuel business earned a profit of $35,000—15 percent of the total operating costs of running the agency. For this coming year, it is projected that this amount will increase to $50,000. Over time, it may be realistic to expect the fuel business to support half of HDC's costs.

It is important to remember that HDC's venture was, again, a case where earned income was a "lucky by-product," and not the original motivation. It is also a case where only by incurring a large debt did the fuel business attract attention to itself and force greater administrative controls, which have led to a more efficient operation. HDC is now considering the separate incorporation of the fuel business.

FOOD FOR PEOPLE

Food-Buying Service

Food for People is a nonprofit organization that focuses on food and nutrition issues in New York City. Several years ago it "backed into" a business venture when it appeared that many day care and senior centers in the poorer areas of the city were having difficulty purchasing fruits and vegetables at a reasonable price. Food for People decided to investigate a business to meet this need. A subsequent feasibility study confirmed that there was a market. It also showed that Food for People could beat wholesalers' prices by up to 22 percent and effect up to 50 percent in savings for groups, in comparison to supermarket prices. Food for People felt that not only would it be performing a valuable service, but that this buying service could eventually earn enough money to subsidize the advocacy work of the parent organization. An important additional factor was the promise of a $35,000 interest-free loan from a major foundation, and numerous offers of free technical consultation.

A project director was selected, as well as a professional buyer at Hunts Point fruit and vegetable market in the South Bronx. In addition, a driver and helper and an administrative staff were hired to take orders and do outreach. An eighteen-foot truck was rented.

The venture looked promising in the beginning. Within a few months, 75 customers were being served, and quality produce delivered. However, sales were much lower than had been projected. Second-year sales totaled $217,000, as compared to a projected $760,000. However, staff kept hoping that, with additional outreach, they could substantially raise the volume of sales. By the beginning of the third year, it was clear that the initial sales projections had been completely unrealistic. The buying service could only earn 35 percent of its costs, and fund raising was necessary to make up the difference. This provoked a crisis for the board, which began to question the overall logic that had pushed Food for People to start a business.

Research showed that the market had changed over three years. Produce wholesalers had become conglomerates, selling all kinds of products in addition to fruits and vegetables. This meant that small centers previously unable to meet minimum-order requirements could now order all types of products and meet minimums easily. Also, wholesale suppliers had large fleets of trucks and therefore more flexibility in terms of delivery schedules. Since the buying service had only one truck, it could not respond to individual centers' needs. Another major factor was the federal cutbacks in feeding programs under the Reagan administration, which had a devastating impact. These cuts reduced available dollars and forced many centers to switch to frozen or canned products, which were cheaper and much less labor intensive than fresh produce.

Aside from these external shifts, Food for People learned that its market survey had been flawed and that its financial projections had been overly optimistic. Indeed, the buying service began because staff had identified a gap in service, and the assumption had been that the skills of nonprofit staff would be sufficient, as would nonprofit salary scales. As it turned out, the staff had to learn a business they knew absolutely nothing about, and this learning factor was costly. There were other problems that developed out of naiveté and inexperience—poor supervision of the truck operations, reluctance to deal with theft, etc. Moreover, Food for People never factored into its decision the opportunity costs that the buying service would incur. The board had to wonder if subsidizing a buying service was really the best use of foundation money.

The board conducted an evaluation and decided to close the buying service. It felt the business was draining the organization and weakening its primary mission, which was food advocacy. It decided to develop strategies to help social service agencies as an intermediary rather than as a provider of direct services. It also concluded that Food for People was not ready to create the kind of entrepreneurial conditions that a business seemed to necessitate.

FEMINIST FILMMAKERS

Distribution Service

Feminist Filmmakers is a nonprofit media center that facilitates the production, promotion, and distribution of films and videotapes by independent women producers. It is the only women's media organization in the United States that provides comprehensive services to women producers of media as well as those organizations who use media in their educational and community programs. Feminist Filmmakers carries out a range of projects to achieve its objectives: technical assistance, a film distribution service, a newsletter, and a speaker's bureau.

Like most other small nonprofits, Feminist Filmmakers started out in 1972 with the assumption that it would be largely supported by government contracts and private foundation grants. However, after twice being defunded, Feminist Filmmakers realized that it had to rely more on its own ability to raise income, or it wouldn't be able to survive the constant cash flow crises. It began to put more effort into building up its film distribution service, which staff felt could eventually pay a significant amount of the expenses of the office.

The film distribution service was inherently problematic, since the films that were being produced and marketed were films that were not commercially viable and for which there was a very limited audience. This was the reason a nonprofit organization had first come into existence—to provide a forum by which these unmarketable films could be seen. To make enough money from the distribution service to subsidize the newsletter and technical assistance services would have necessitated a radical restructuring in the kinds of films that were bought and rented through the service.

At first, no one realized the dilemma. On paper it looked as if the distribution service was growing. Its income increased 25 percent in 1984; however, its costs—shipping, lab, promotion, royalties, staff—were more than twice the rental and sales fees! In fact, the government contracts to do training with community groups were subsidizing the distribution service.

A consultant was soon hired to evaluate the growth potential of the distribution service. She concluded that, in order to make any profit, the organization would have to change its name, broaden its library of topics relevant to women, and drop all films that did not net more than $1,000 a year. This last step would mean getting rid of 95 percent of the current library. A final decision has yet to be made.

LESSONS FROM THE CASE STUDIES

The previous cases do not present one clear-cut model for enterprise for small nonprofits. There are successes and failures. The successes, however, are modest while the failures often border on the disastrous. It pays to look more closely at what the experiences of these ten organizations tell us about the hazards of enterprise.

The first two cases, Call for Food and Clark Henry Development Corporation, could be viewed as extensions of grassroots fund-raising strategies. For years, nonprofits have been selling buttons and T-shirts without thinking of them as earned income or enterprise. It has been considered a piece of a fund-raising strategy. What has changed in the 1980s is that organizations are more serious about looking for sales revenue because other funding sources have dried up. This raises the ante for them in an important new way. The new factor is the need for greater expertise in the areas of management and marketing. This is a big part of the dilemma the small nonprofit faces.

Many directors of small organizations have little or no management background, and marketing is something that, until very recently, was considered irrelevant. All of the directors in the cases presented here started as either social workers or community organizers. Their reason for running a nonprofit organization is an issue-based one. They did not take their jobs because they enjoyed administering an agency.

Besides the lack of marketing expertise, several other factors hinder the growth of enterprise in small nonprofits. First, there is a board of directors, who by law function as the policy makers of the corporation. They have to be consulted throughout the earned income process, and they can slow down decision making significantly. Second, there is an attitude toward money and profit making that is hard to reform. The culture of nonprofits is not as "hard-nosed" as for-profits, and their first priority is *always* seen as the issue their organization was set up to address. Indeed, many nonprofits are used to giving away their services for free.

Third, most small nonprofits have little more than a rough idea of what their internal costs are. This was true for all the organizations described earlier. How much does it cost the director to spend two hours on the phone with a corporation that has some typewriters to donate? What does it cost to have a three-hour staff meeting? What does that desk in the corner cost to leave vacant? Is it really cheaper to walk the five blocks to the post office every two weeks rather than rent a postal meter? These are the types of questions that the typical director of a small nonprofit has difficulty answering. This kind of information is essential when it comes to figuring out how to charge a fee-for-service.

Community Resource Exchange, a former employer of the author, is a useful case in point. In 1981, CRE was asked by a foundation officer what it would charge per hour if it offered us a contract for service rather than a grant. The staff had no idea. Each made a guess, which ranged from $15 to $60. To get the answer, the staff members kept records of how they spent their time for six months. The data were compiled and common categories were established. But categories kept changing, which meant that CRE had no consistent base of information. So it kept time records for another six months. By the end of a year the staff had a figure: $50 per hour. Most were shocked by how high the figure was.

This process of record keeping helped CRE to become more efficient in how its employees spent their time. When it found that staff meetings were costing us $2,000 a month, the number and the length were reduced. At bottom, CRE found that it was providing a service that effectively priced it out of the marketplace. It could only continue if the subsidy by corporations and foundations was increased, if it cut its costs, or if it combined the two options.

This is a complicated issue for the small nonprofit. Many of the organizations presented here were set up to provide services to a population that may have little ability to pay fees. If the nonprofit begins to charge for its services, it may well change its clientele, and in so doing, perhaps, destroy its reason for existing. Not all nonprofits are suitable for enterprise, as Feminist Filmmakers and Food for People make clear. Their mission demands a third-party payer's participation.

The need to earn income is pushing many nonprofits to scrutinize their operations. The good news is that almost all of them can benefit from some analysis of their costs. Many nonprofits have long skirted the issue of productivity, and it may be that cost analysis will compel them to attend to it more seriously. For once a nonprofit puts itself into the market, it has to deal with the twin issues of cost and productivity. In short, it opens itself up to the kind of evaluation that any small business faces. Will the customer buy the product or service? Why? Why not? In all the cases presented here, the directors learned something from their attempts to answer these questions.

The organizations that were relatively successful at charging fees were organizations like Equal Employment for Women and Children's Advocate, which had services that corporations could purchase. They were able to charge for those services without any important changes in their mission. What happened, in effect, was that they expanded their services into different market segments.

Other organizations that were successful at earning some income were those like the Clearinghouse for the Institutionalized Aged that had their first effort largely paid for by a foundation; start-up costs were low. This is important because learning is an expensive process, often too expensive for small nonprofits. However, once an expertise is developed and a market for a product identified, the potential for income increases.

Two of the most successful cases—Project Open Door and the Housing Development Council—must be considered qualified successes because their earned income ventures took them away from their stated missions. Project Open Door, which was set up to fight housing discrimination, now runs a corporate placement program. The Housing Development Council's original objective, to provide low-cost fuel to low-income housing projects, has been altered. It now exclusively markets its services to affluent homeowners. This is not to say that these two organizations made bad decisions. Both have been able to use the earned income to subsidize their organizing work.

As suggested above, it is important for both staff and board to understand the marketplace and the potential for charging fees-for-service. Not all nonprofits can be rescued by resorting to that marketplace for fees, of course. But it is an important alternative to consider, and the process by which a nonprofit comes to a decision regarding fees is one that is certain to strengthen the management capability of that organization.

Starting an entirely new business, like Food for People did, is a much riskier and less likely alternative for the small nonprofit. First, the time to learn the business might be too long to produce success. Second, very few foundations will make grants for capital expenses, if such money is needed. This was a problem for Kids Care. Its thrift shop had potential, but it had no money to invest in renting a storefront and making capital improvements. Third, all new earned income ventures need time to prove themselves, and the small nonprofit may not have the cash resources to wait until the venture turns a profit. And, because of their nature and size, traditional sources of capital, like banks, will be loathe to lend money.

Annotated Bibliography

Abramson, Alan J., and M. Salamon, Lester. *The Nonprofit Sector and the New Federal Budget.* Washington, D.C.: Urban Institute Press, 1986.

A very comprehensive and extremely important book of findings on the condition of the voluntary sector in the Reagan era. The findings are revealing and disturbing.

Business Planning Guide: A Handbook to Help You Design, Write and Use a Business Plan and a Financing Proposal. Dover, N.H.: Upstart Publishing Co., 1979.

Absolutely the best guide to preparing a business plan, using the establishment of a local, retail fish market as the case in point. (The cost is $15.20 prepaid, to Upstart Publishing Co., 50 Mill Street, Dover, NH 03820).

Crimmins, James C., and Keil, Mary. *Enterprise in the Nonprofit Sector.* Washington, D.C.: Partners for Liveable Places, 1983.

The only study based on survey data of tax-exempt 501(c)(3) groups, this book is readable and provocative, suggesting new tax and organizational strategies for nonprofit organizations. (The cost is $7.00 prepaid, to Publishing Center for Cultural Resources, 625 Broadway, New York, NY 10012)

Hopkins, Bruce R. "Tax Implications of Profit-Making Ventures," *Grantsmanship Center News,* vol. 10, 1983, pp. 38–41.

A very informed introduction to tax law and earned income ventures by one of the best-known lawyers in the field.

Kotler, Philip. *Marketing for Nonprofit Organizations.* Second Edition. Englewood Cliffs, N.J.: Prentice-Hall, 1982.

This is a superior marketing textbook containing many nonprofit examples. Very solid and a little dry.

Kuriloff, Arthur H., and Hemphill, John M., Jr. *How to Start Your Own Business . . . and Succeed.* Revised edition. New York, N.Y.: McGraw Hill, 1981.

One of many how-to books, this one is especially useful for its worksheets and individual "tests." Also, it is strong on business planning and has a good appendix describing a bookstore venture.

Lovelock, Christopher H., and Weinberg, Charles B. *Marketing for Public and Nonprofit Managers.* Second edition. Redwood City, CA: The Scientific Press, 1988.

Absolutely the best text book on the subject; comprehensive and a pleasure to read.

New York State Department of Commerce, *Your Business: A Management Guide for Small Business,* Albany, N.Y.: Division for Small Business.

A very useful basic guide for starting and running a small business, with some very useful statistics on start-ups (by subsector). Uncommonly good, particularly for a government publication.

Phillips, Michael, and Raspberry, Sally. *Honest Business: A Superior Strategy for Starting and Managing Your Own Business.* New York, N.Y.: Random House, 1981.

This is a very wise and simple statement showing how ethics and business can mix, and mix well. Solid advice on key aspects of business. Phillips is a successful banker turned new-age entrepreneur and author.

Rich, Stanley R., and Gumpert, David E. *Business Plans That Win $$$,* New York, N.Y.: Harper & Row, 1985.

This is an artfully written, nonquantitative guide to business plans, from the point of view of what potential investors look for. It is one of the best books of advice on the market.

Skloot, Edward. "Enterprise and Commerce in Nonprofit Organizations," in *The Nonprofit Sector: A Research Handbook,* ed. by Walter W. Powell. New Haven, Ct.: Yale University Press, 1987.

A comprehensive discussion of the history and likely future of nonprofit enterprise. Contains four case studies, discusses operational and legal problems, and highlights fundamental issues relating to competition within and between the sectors.

Skloot, Edward. "Should Not-for-Profits Go Into Business?" *Harvard Business Review,* vol. 61, 1983, pp. 20–27.

A short statement about what nonprofit organizations need to do in order to make it in business.

Troyer, Thomas A., and Boisture, Robert A. "Charities and the Fiscal Crisis: Creative Approaches to Income Production," and Mark D. Turkel, "Business Activities (Related and Unrelated) of Tax Exempt Organizations and Their Tax Consequences," both in *Proceedings of the New York University Thirteenth Conference on Charitable Organizations.* Albany, N.Y.: Matthew Bender, 1983.

Two excellent articles in a hard-to-get volume.

U. S. Small Business Administration, *Unfair Competition By Nonprofit Organizations with Small Business: An Issue for the 1980s.* Washington, D.C.: Office of the Chief Counsel for Advocacy, 1983.

This is the SBA broadside that has caused much concern in the nonprofit/philan-thropic community. It takes isolated cases and elevates them to systemic problems. Controversial, and deservedly so.

White, Richard M., Jr. *The Entrepreneur's Manual: Business Start-ups, Spin-Offs, and Innovative Management.* Radnor, Pa.: Chilton, 1977.

A no-nonsense, superbly arranged, practical book by a consultant-entrepreneur. It concentrates on for-profit issues, but there is much carryover.

Wiewel, Wim, et al. *Business Spin-Offs: Planning the Organization of Business Activities.* University of Illinois at Chicago Circle: Center for Urban Economic Development, 1982.

A very thoughtful and useful book (partially represented in this volume) on the advantages and disadvantages of for-profit/nonprofit and separate/in-house opera-tions. Many useful case examples from the Chicago LDC/CDC community.

Williams, Roger. "Why Don't We Start a Profit Making Subsidiary," *Grantsmanship Center News.* vol. 10, 1983, pp. 14–23.

A good, quick overview of opportunities and pitfalls in nonprofit entrepreneurship.

Index